An alliance of misfits.
We fight evil by talking
about what we love.

Publisher/Editor in Chief: Marjorie Steele
Illustrator: Dustin Coon
Proof Editor: Jason Rehmus

Special thanks to: Nancy Hildebrandt, the Fairy Godmother of Wordpress and wise crone to wayward mothers, without whose loving, practical, and eucatastrophically well-timed magic we'd have a bunch of books and nowhere to sell them. It's good to have a fairy godmother.

Published by COSGRRRL, a @creativeonion Press publication, in Michigan, 2021.

ISBN: 978-1-7345816-3-8

The Elemental Series
Issue #2: Mind / Air

Actually, U really need to UNLEARN as much as possible.
U need to UNLEARN what U have LEARNED so U kan
RELEARN all that U have FORGOTTEN.

- Reverend Nigga Daddy

TABLE OF CONTENTS

Elemental, Issue #2: Mind / Air

A NOTE FROM THE PUBLISHER
Why this magazine's name is feminine, but its content isn't

When I launched COSGRRRL in 2017—a digital nerd magazine which aims to fight evil by creating a platform for people from all backgrounds to talk about what they love and why it matters—I knew that the name would throw a lot of people. I knew there would be some confusion about exactly who COSGRRRL is targeting, and the perspective of its content.

Specifically: I knew that a lot of people would assume by "grrrl" that the publication focuses on women's issues, or at least on women's voices specifically.

It doesn't. The editorial scope, as you may notice, is extremely broad, ranging from PC game reviews to fanfiction to cospoetry, with the only common denominators being that they answer the question: what do you love, and why does it matter?

That's it. It's based on a simple (well researched, I might add) thesis:

When we talk with each other about what we love, we make the world a better place—and sci-fi and fantasy are uniquely equipped to get us talking about things that truly matter.

I've published men and women from a variety of backgrounds, from home-schooled Christian to anti-capitalist political activist. That broad scope is intentional. It's kind of the whole bit. It's bringing together different people to express what they love.

The fact that some people assume by the magazine's name that it has a gendered—and therefore niche—focus…I actually kind of like that. Because it gives me something interesting to turn upside down.

And I really like turning things upside down. I think we need a lot more of that. That's why I launched COSGRRRL.

There are plenty of male-gendered brand names with products that have nothing to do with gender. Simply because it's been the default for a long time. X-Men. League of Extraordinary Gentlemen. Men with Pens, a copywriting agency which was ironically founded by a woman.

So I'd like us to challenge the default. If The X-Men have Jean Gray, why can't COSGRRRL have Reverend Nigga Daddy and Bill Henning?

Being a **COSGRRRL**, in my view, has nothing to do with your gender, and everything to do with your willingness to share what you love—and why it matters.

COSGRRRL mascot by Kyle DeVries

!
?
CRITICAL FAILURE

Essays

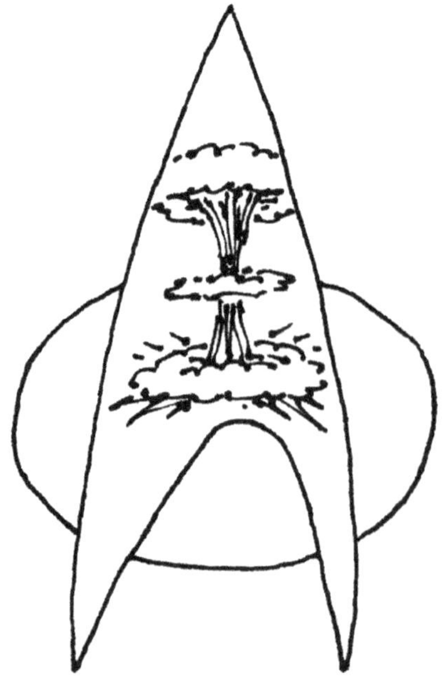

'Star Trek VI:' A Cold War Allegory

A history lesson in cowboy diplomacy

by Richard Brownell

Two great powers have warily stared each other down from across a vast, deadly space for generations. One side is for the most part benevolent, open, and free, offering people the power of self-determination. The other is secretive and militaristic, constantly seeking territorial expansion using force and subjugation.

For generations, they have competed for the souls of all peoples, using technology, politics, culture, and propaganda to prove their superiority over their opponents. When that has failed, they have used proxies to fight their battles, but they have always been careful not to engage each other directly. Each side knows their terrible military power would destroy them both if brought to bear.

One day, an incident takes place that unravels the balance of power, and threatens to drag both sides into a devastating conflagration that could cost billions of lives.

If you are a *Star Trek* fan, you would recognize right away that this is the premise for *Star Trek VI: The Undiscovered Country*. If you are a history buff, you would say, hey, this sounds a lot like the final years of the Cold War between the United States and the Soviet Union.

You're both right.

Aside from being delightfully entertaining, *Star Trek* has always been great for offering cogent social commentary. From the days of the original series in the late 1960s on up through the films and TV spinoffs that began in the 1980s, *Star Trek* has explored all the elements of the human condition.

Some of the most memorable episodes are those that force the characters to confront war, racism, xenophobia, greed, environmental degradation; all in a way that resonated with viewers.

Star Trek was a creation of the 1960s, and influenced by events of the era.

All the tragedy and turmoil of that time helped feed the storylines of the show. The civil rights struggles, the Vietnam War, the unbridgeable generation gap, and particularly the Cold War were all put through a sci-fi lens by some of the top writers in the genre.

The Cold War between the United States and the Soviet Union filled many people with dread. Fear of an unknown enemy, fear of being dominated by a foreign power, and fear of global annihilation was shared by Americans and Russians alike.

In *Star Trek*, the Cold War as we knew it was ancient history, but the Federation was in the midst of a similar conflict with the Klingon Empire — Gene Roddenberry's stand-in for the Soviet Union. An aggressive, militaristic species bent on territorial gain, the Klingons shot first and asked questions never. It was often up to the quick-thinking Captain Kirk and the crew of the Enterprise to outwit the Klingons and keep the fragile peace on both sides of the Neutral Zone, the 23rd century equivalent of the Berlin Wall.

The Klingons would pop in and out of storylines in the original series and the films that followed, raising an intergalactic ruckus that sometimes shadowed events in our modern world. *Star Trek VI: The Undiscovered Country* is the most obvious instance of this.

The final film to feature the original crew of the Enterprise, *Star Trek VI* originated from a question posed by Leonard Nimoy, "What if the Wall came down in space?" The Berlin Wall had been torn down in 1989, with the collapse of the Communist Bloc following over the next couple of years. It was a good time to be alive, but it was also a time when anything could happen. The Soviets could pursue peace with the West, or in the words of Spock referring to the Klingons, they might "attempt a military solution and die fighting."

Star Trek VI opens with the massive explosion of an energy facility on the Klingon moon, Praxis. The Klingons downplay the incident and refuse Federation assistance, but it's evident that this tragedy is a major issue for the Empire. It signifies their industrial and military weakness and inability to provide for their people.

The Praxis incident was inspired by the 1986 nuclear accident at Chernobyl in the Ukraine. It was a major catastrophe that the Soviets tried to hide but failed after radiation drifted across much of Europe. At the height of the Cold War in the 1980s, Chernobyl became a symbol of crumbling Soviet infrastructure, and it came at a time when Russia's new leader, Mikhail Gorbachev, was upsetting the political status quo with his outreach to America. Gorbachev represented a new path for relations between the U.S. and the Soviets, but communist hardliners didn't see it that way.

The Star Trek equivalent to Gorbachev was Klingon Chancellor Gorkon who, after Praxis, proposes to open negotiations with the Federation to dismantle starbases and outposts along the Neutral Zone. Kirk and the Enterprise are assigned to escort Gorkon to Earth for the talks. Gorkon's peaceful ambitions prove too much for Chang, his militaristic chief of staff, who concocts a complicated plot with Federation traitors to assassinate Gorkon before he reaches Earth. Kirk, along with Dr. McCoy of all people, is arrested for the crime and sent to Kronos, the Klingon home world, for trial.

While nothing as drastic as an assassination took place to keep Gorbachev from signing an historic arms treaty with the U.S. to remove all nuclear missiles from Europe, there was a coup in 1991 by old guard communists to remove him from power. They feared Gorbachev's policies would lead to an end to the communist state, so they locked him up in a dacha in the Crimea and declared a state of emergency. The plotters proved inept at executing their plan, and the Russian people protested in the streets. The coup failed and by the end of 1991, shortly after *Star Trek VI* premiered, the Soviet Union dissolved.

There are several historical tidbits sprinkled throughout *Star Trek VI* that relate to the Cold War. During a dinner aboard the Enterprise, before the manure hits the air circulator, Gorkon and his Klingon cohorts muse with Kirk and crew over what the future holds. Amid quotes from Shakespeare and Adolf Hitler, the dialogue resembles the debates of the late 1980s and early 1990s as to what might become of a post-Cold War world.

The trial of Kirk and McCoy also has a moment that is lost to all but the most hardcore history buffs. During Chang's examination of Kirk on the witness stand, he tries to set Kirk up by asking if he was obeying or disobeying orders when he assassinated Gorkon. He shouts at Kirk,

"DON'T WAIT FOR THE TRANSLATION. ANSWER ME NOW."

This is the line American Ambassador to the U.N. Adlai Stevenson delivered to Soviet Ambassador Valerian Zorin during the Cuban Missile Crisis in 1962. "Do you deny that the U.S.S.R. has placed, and is placing, medium- and intermediate-range missiles and sites in Cuba? Yes or no — don't wait for the translation — yes or no?"

And then there is the classic line which is my personal favorite of the whole film. When Captain Kirk, scourge of the Klingons, protests at being appointed to escort Gorkon to Earth, Spock reminds him of the old Vulcan proverb:

"ONLY NIXON COULD GO TO CHINA."

This alludes to staunch anti-communist Richard Nixon's historic 1972 trip to Communist China to normalize relations between the two nations. Spock's point being that a peace overture could only be taken seriously if the toughest man on the block is the one to offer it.

Star Trek VI ends with Kirk, Spock, and crew saving the day and riding off into the sunset. The movie was a big hit and went on to become a fan favorite, in part because it was marketed during *Star Trek*'s 25th anniversary as the last voyage of the original Enterprise crew. Like all the best science fiction stories, though, *The Undiscovered Country* also offered an opportunity to comment and reflect on our contemporary world in a way that was entertaining and thought-provoking at the same time. It even snuck in a history lesson or two, and that's always a good thing.

"Infinity War" + the Gordian Knot of 'The Greater Good'

What happens when a giant film franchise takes its closest look at the notion of 'greater good'?

by Sarah Myles

With *Avengers: Infinity War*, Marvel has taken a further step into the depths of the idea of personal sacrifice for 'the greater good.' This has long been a popular theme for Hollywood, featuring prominently in just about every genre — from horror and drama, to comedy and science fiction — and usually takes the form of 'greater' meaning 'for the benefit of more people.' Think of Spock's iconic line:

"The good of the many outweigh the good of the few — or the one."

Even Westerns are often run through with the thread of the responsibility of the few to serve the need of the many.

It should come as no surprise. It is the noble lot of heroism, after all — and that is, rather ironically, the bread and butter of the Hollywood studio hierarchy. But, in practice, what does it actually mean when such an industry focuses its idea of heroism on such a narrow definition?

The Marvel Cinematic Universe is a movie enterprise of gigantic proportion. With 19 films released so far over 10 years, costing over $3.6 billion in collective budget, this franchise has already earned over $15.4 billion in global box office. That figure is set to rise quickly and steeply with *Avengers: Infinity War* now on general release around the world. This means that the Marvel Cinematic Universe is the highest grossing film series in history — easily out stripping *Star Wars*, *Harry Potter*, *James Bond*, *The Lord Of The Rings*, *Transformers*, *The Fast And The Furious*, and *Mission: Impossible*.

From the achievement of this lofty status, we can surmise that the reach of the Marvel Cinematic Universe, in terms of pop culture influence, is unparalleled. Again, this should come as no surprise, since the franchise does reside within the stable of Disney properties, and the Disney brand dominates the world in terms of pop culture influence. There is a case to be made, then, that it's important that we apply a critical eye to the messages of these movies, which are so enthusiastically beloved of adults and children alike, all over the world.

The greater good: what does it mean?

At the heart of every instalment in this franchise lies the idea of self sacrifice for the 'greater good.' Iron Man has to learn the importance of it over the course of his own solo movies — the third of which centers on the PTSD he suffers from in the aftermath of trying to sacrifice himself for the residents of Manhattan, in 2012's Avengers. The Incredible Hulk is all about the 'greater good,' as he tries to prevent his rage monster from damaging innocent lives, while also trying to prevent the U.S government from weaponising his anger management issue against humans. Thor has to overcome his own selfishness and take responsibility for the people of Asgard (and the universe) — sacrificing his chance at love.

Captain America literally sacrifices himself to save the world, by flying his aircraft into the ice in 2011's *Captain America: The First Avenger* — then sacrifices his worldview in 2014's *The Winter Soldier,* and his reputation in 2016's *Civil War*. In 2014's *Guardians Of The Galaxy*, the newly formed team of outcasts ultimately share the burden of sacrifice, as Peter Quill and friends take the full force of an Infinity Stone. In 2015's *Avengers: Age Of Ultron*, the team is prepared to sacrifice themselves for the people of Sokovia, before Pietro Maximoff does indeed sacrifice himself for a young boy.

Ant-Man is willing to sacrifice himself for the good of his child and the rest of the world, while Doctor Strange sacrifices his impressive ego to become a protector of dimensions and the mystic arts. 2017's *Guardians Of The Galaxy Vol 2* saw Yondu Udonta sacrifice himself to save the rest of the team — and specifically his adopted son Peter Quill — after Peter had been prepared to sacrifice himself to save the universe from his biological father, Ego. *Spider-Man: Homecoming* sees Peter Parker prepare to sacrifice himself to save the world from Avengers technology when it seems it might fall into the wrong hands. Thor literally sacrifices his home to save his people from his sister in 2017's *Thor: Ragnarok*, and T'Challa is repeatedly prepared to sacrifice himself for the people and future of Wakanda, in 2018's *Black Panther*. Not only does he, as king, constantly place himself on the front line of conflict — with Ulysses Klaue and Erik Killmonger — he literally relinquishes the power of the Black Panther in order to uphold cultural law, resulting in his defeat in conflict with Killmonger.

The twist

And then, there's *Avengers: Infinity War* — about which the Disney marketing machine has declared, "It all leads to this." Each of these characters has learned about sacrifice over the past decade, and all of that understanding is brought to bear upon the group in this latest series chapter. In addition to the general air of personal sacrifice — with Thor and Peter Quill comparing losses, and each character charging into battle with nary a thought for their own safety — three specific heroes in three specific situations make the same demand of a fellow hero: when it comes to it, you have to kill me.

Each situation presents a different dynamic. Vision bears the Mind Stone in his forehead, but is romantically involved with Scarlet Witch. Thanos is coming for the Stone and, if he achieves his goal, he can wipe out half the population of the universe in a heartbeat. Vision tells Scarlet Witch to destroy the Mind Stone in his head, as she is the only being on the planet powerful enough to do so. Gamora — the adopted daughter of Thanos — knows that he is coming, and makes Peter Quill promise to kill her to prevent Thanos from taking her. Gamora and Peter are romantically involved, but Gamora knows that in Thanos' hands the knowledge she has of the Soul stone's location poses a risk to everyone in the Universe. Doctor Strange assures Iron Man that he will not hesitate to kill him and Spider-Man, if he has to choose between them, and saving the universe. They are trapped together in the home of Thanos, and anticipate a difficult battle upon his arrival — as Doctor Strange has the Time Stone.

For a variety of reasons, each of those heroes hesitates to sacrifice a loved one/colleague. Those promises are broken, and the consequences are utterly, utterly devastating — on a universal scale. On the other hand, in essentially the same scenario, Thanos does not hesitate to sacrifice a loved one — and he achieves his goal. This is pivotal when it comes to this movie getting its point across.
Perhaps more than any other instalment in the Marvel Cinematic Universe, this heavy construction of a film seems determined to tell us something. These heroes that we have repeatedly congregated to celebrate over the course of a decade have been brought together here for a very specific purpose. Thanos himself is given a great deal of screen time, and his character is fleshed out in a way that no other Marvel villain has been before. He is a genocidal tyrant, certainly — but he has become convinced of the virtue of his own delusions, and the strength of his personal convictions makes him both terrifying, and oddly persuasive, in the way that all abusive men are.

And this is where the conflict lies — in the notion of 'the greater good.' This is the Gordian Knot at the heart of the franchise narrative.

It all leads to this.
When both the heroes and the villain believe they are working in the interests of 'the greater good,' things appear very complicated indeed. The whole thing hinges on their respective interpretation of what 'the greater good' actually is. In this instance, the heroes are fighting for the status quo, while Thanos is fighting for change. Thanos believes he can bring order and bal-

ance to the universe by snapping half of it out of existence. The Avengers and their allies disagree — believing that to be a cruel and unnecessary act.

Of course, our heroes are correct. Much as Thanos attempts to justify his position with 'reasoned' argument, his interpretation of 'the greater good' is fundamentally flawed because — as is revealed through flashbacks — he has long travelled through space, arriving in population centres and slaughtering the halves that oppose him. His knowledge of the Infinity Stones merely provides him the opportunity to take that strategy to a universal level, instantaneously. He is, in truth, a megalomaniac, seeking only the power to oppress on a wider scale.

Clearly, this is destined to also be his undoing because, by achieving his goal, he did not sort his opposition from the compliant and submissive, as he had previously done on a smaller canvas— leaving a great many motivated enemies still to face.

But, as complex as this situation may appear, this Gordian Knot is sliced through in the end by the very clear depiction of the fact that while the phrase 'the greater good' sounds as though it has a moral implication, its definition is variable within the human experience. It is, in fact, determined by whoever is most powerful at any given time. The winners write the history books. As unpleasant as it is, this has always been the case — as those that have invoked the sacred 'greater good' in their public rhetoric have invariably meant, 'What's good for me and mine.'

This is true of our heroes here, too. Thanos achieving his goal is not good for them — it is only good for his oppressive agenda. Though he talks about bringing order and balance, the act of blinking half of the population out of the universe brings nothing but chaos and destruction. As heroes, this significantly increases their workload, while potentially diminishing their number — in addition to being objectively morally and ethically wrong. For them, the 'greater good' is definitely the status quo — in other words, none of the universe being erased, and everything trundling along, just as it always has.

It makes for fascinating interrogation, though. In our real inequitable global society, it is always the oppressors and aggressors that argue in favour of the status quo. In a patriarchal social structure that favours wealthy white people above all others, it is never those that wish to rock the boat and make change that get to call the real and effective shots. Rather, it is those sympathetic to the needs of the men at the top of that hierarchy — and thus, that hierarchy is perpetuated. In this way, the reality of 'the greater good' — as opposed to the fictional, Hollywood version — is not noble at all. The only personal sacrifice it requires is of one's morality.

So, what is *Avengers: Infinity War* saying on this subject? That it's better the devilish status quo you know? As our heroes defend a cruel and inequitable universe from something even worse, are we to understand that the argument here is to fight off the bigger threat to life, and we can work on the rest of that pesky oppression later?

Of course it is, because that's the way the world works — and in that respect, our Avengers certainly are supporting the status quo. Since the beginning of time, there has always been a reason not to address social inequity. There is always something else — something far more important and urgent — to be dealt with. In today's politics, it is usually terrorism, or a fight purposefully picked with another nation that requires the oppressed to wait for their liberation.

These are the strategies that allow those in power to line the pockets of their arms-investing peers living in safety, while the less fortunate — living in the firing line — are expected to make their sacrifice for 'the greater good.' This makes *Avengers: Infinity War* an on-brand cautionary tale — as the hesitation of certain heroes in making their required sacrifice paves the way for 'something even worse.'

"IT ALL LEADS TO THIS."

Yes, Marvel. It always, always does.

Modeling the Socioeconomic Future with Dungeons and Dragons

Gary Gygax: (1), Charles Murray: (0), Artificial Intelligence: (?)

by BJ Campbell

When I get too fed up with the relative noise level in the media about whether Charles Murray is or isn't racist, or James Damore is or isn't misogynist, or the coming wave of Artificial Intelligence is or isn't going to destroy humanity, I crack open a cold beer with a few friends and play Dungeons and Dragons.

The first big reason nobody thinks of Dungeons and Dragons, the ultimately nerdy tabletop roleplaying game, as racist, is because it has different "races" than we do. There's no differentiation between nationalities or ethnicities in it, and unless you're climbing to the top of the pile of nerds to build a Drow (dark elf) character, there's no accounting for skin color in it either. It does, however, dive deeply into the idea that different players' characters, or "PCs," have different levels of aptitude at doing different stuff. The game calls these "ability scores," and the distribution of natural aptitude in these ability scores is set on none other than a classic bell curve.

YOLO

Let's suppose one day you wake up and decide to live the nerd life. You bust out a blank character sheet, which looks like something you'll have to search DuckDuckGo to find yourself, due to copyright restrictions.

You pencil in your hero's name, Doolin the Destroyer or whatever, and you crack out your iconic dice bag. Everybody has a dice bag. They look like bags of gems, with clear or opaque multicolored multifaceted dice, which I think may be part of the allure of the game itself. Makes you feel adventurous. You select three six-sided dice, you roll them, add the results, and get a number somewhere between 3 and 18. You write that in the first box under the ability score for STR—Strength. You repeat for each of the six ability scores, and you discover how good your character is at doing things.

This is a game. This is not real. Let's continue.

Here's what you rolled:
- STR 14
- DEX 7
- CON 12
- INT 7
- WIS 12
- CHA 16

These are pretty good rolls. What do they mean?

Strength represents how strong you are, which is self-explanatory. It will help you climb ropes and bash orcs. This PC should be pretty good at bashing orcs. Dexterity is a measure of fine motor skills and overall coordination, for tight-roping while picking a lock. Constitution is how tough you are, both in terms of your resiliency when being bashed by orcs, and in your endurance and resistance to disease on your forced march through the swamp to avoid the orcs.

Intelligence is how smart you are, at learning languages, disabling complicated Indiana Jones traps in the orc temple of orc doom, or casting spells from a stolen spell book. Wisdom is how sensible, judicious, or crafty you are. While intelligence lets you know it's raining on your forced march through the swamp, wisdom tells you to pitch your tent or you might catch cold. Charisma is a catch-all for your social aptitude, which might include how pretty you are, how funny you are, or how talented you are at that lute you keep carrying around for some reason.

Now you have created a model of a character, a PC, with some dice. Before you select your profession, or "class," you need to think about what this character is going to be good at. This character is strong, resilient, and charming. A fine candidate for a "Paladin," which is a sort of overbearingly lawful, marginally priestly knight, whose classic job in Dungeons and Dragons unfortunately ends up being 80% preventing the "Rogue" character from trying to pick everyone's pocket in the bar, and 20% talking to the town guard after they've apprehended the self-same Rogue.

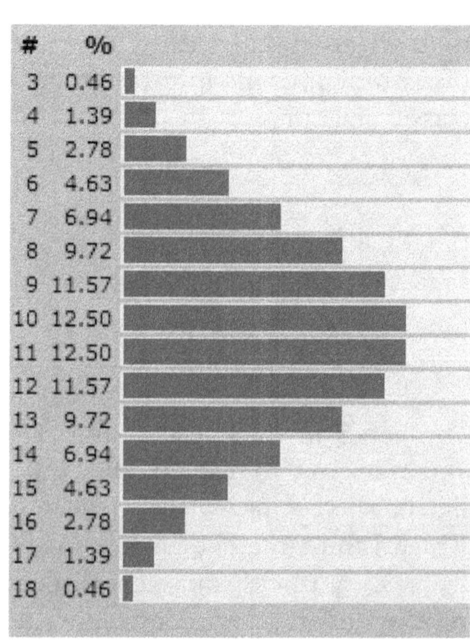

If you're a truly dedicated nerd with a personal Xerox machine, you could make a thousand character sheets, populate them with six thousand sets of die rolls, and the statistical distribution for each statistic would look like this:
This is the classic "3d6" bell curve, generated from adding the results of rolling a six-sided die three times and adding the results.

Wait, Where's the Racism?

Well, here we go. That's the distribution for a human. Dungeons and Dragons, being basically a complicated J.R.R. Tolkien rip-off, has elves, dwarves, halflings, and such as options. And each of these options get a little boost in one stat and a little penalty in another stat.

Doolin the Dwarf would get +2 to his constitution roll, owing to how tough he is, and -2 to his charisma roll, perhaps because dwarves don't often bathe. Whatever. Make a thousand dwarves and here's their charisma distribution:

By the rules of this particular game, the median dwarf has an 8 or 9 charisma, while a median human has a 10 or 11. Does this mean some dwarves aren't charming? No, it does not. Does this mean if you meet a Dwarf on the street you should automatically presume he's a social oaf?

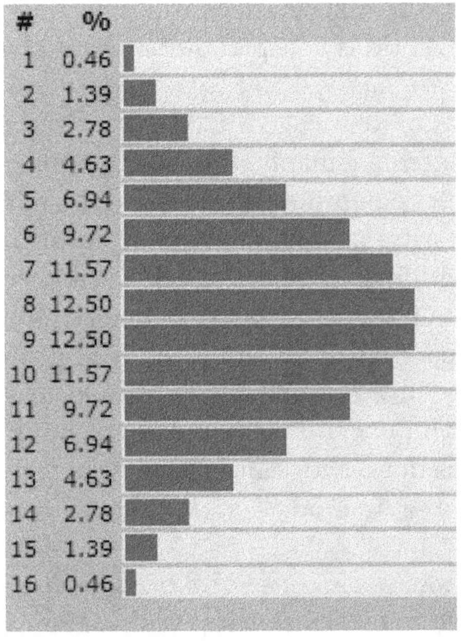

Only if you're racist. Here's what it does mean. 50% of humans have an 11 or better, while 25.93% of dwarves have an 11 or better. A dwarf in the top 5% of all dwarves (14) would find himself in the top 16% of humans in the same statistic. This is how we properly speak of population level statistical differences in an ability score, for this completely concocted, not at all real game.

Now the second (and more important) reason nobody thinks Dungeons and Dragons is racist. Even though there are population level statistical differences in races in Dungeons and Dragons, there's no one race that's objectively better than another one at the overall game. Any of them can be good at any profession, be it Warrior or Rogue or Priest or Wizard or the rest, depending on the dice. But certain races tend to end up in certain professions owing to the statistical bonuses laid out in the rules. All the different professions available are useful in your adventures, so there's no race that's just garbage and not worth playing.

Meet the Shitty Dungeon Master

All Dungeons and Dragons nerds have had a shitty dungeon master at
some point. The dungeon master (DM) is the story teller, who plays all the
non-player characters, sets up the story, sends you on quests, and generally
builds a game session, or series of game sessions, into a reasonable facsimile
of an original JRR Tolkien rip-off novel. A good one will spin an elaborate
yarn whereby your characters start out as nobodies and end as great and
renowned heroes.

But you ended up with a shitty one this time. And I mean the worst.

First off, in his game world there's no orcs. Not a one. No dragons either.
The world is conspicuously bereft of monsters. "We still get to fight, right?"
Oh yes, he says, you get to fight other people. "Whew." But, he says, hun-
dreds of years ago a Court Mage by the name of Barron le Bourgeoys
invented a cheaply reproducible magic stick that kills people at range, much
better than a bow, so nobody uses swords or bows anymore. All it takes is
dexterity, and perhaps a little constitution if you have to march across the
Kingdom of Ahlissa on your military campaign. "Can I be a blacksmith?"
Certainly not, he says. All blacksmithing is done by magic golems now,
which are tireless, and owned by a small cloister of merchant wizards who
know how to build them. "What the hell, dude, I have a Strength character
over here, can I at least, like, farm or something?" Oh no, he replies, farm-
ing is done with elaborate self-propelled gnomish contraptions and the world
has infinite food.

So now you're pissed off because the character you've got rolled up and
ready to go is pure crap in this game world, all the while Joe over there
(screw you Joe) is giggling all the way to the bank, because his character
has a high Intelligence. His wizard is going to learn to craft golems. You're
screwed, Joe's not, and this game isn't going to be very much fun at all. Be
glad you brought a six pack.

This is what Charles Murray's book *The Bell Curve* is mostly about.

"The Bell Curve"

I'm not going to get deep in the weeds defending this book, because if you
want to argue about the book's validity, or methodology, or politics, there is
a near infinite amount of other stuff you could read that's much more com-
plete than I could ever pray to do. It might be right, it might be garbage,
but I increasingly believe its relative position on the rightness-garbage scale
won't matter anyway, in the not-too-distant future. To understand why, let's
lay out some of the positions he took, restated in the terms of our Dungeons
and Dragons model.

1. Your INT ability score (for him, IQ) is basically static, and you can't really increase it.
2. Your INT is noticeably "heritable," a term with which you should familiarize yourself.
3. Our economy is currently and increasingly rigged so that INT is way more important than all the other stats, if you're trying to get rich or powerful.
4. This is going to create a situation where a small number of highly intelligent technocrats are going to end up concentrating a disproportionately large amount of the wealth.
5. There's a racial bonus to INT.

While #1 is certainly debatable, that #5 is the sticky part, and it's the part that gets Murray called either a racist, or a bad scientist, and I'm not going to take a position on that discussion at all. Could be neither, or one, or the other, or both. But we have to admit that there are measured differences between the IQ of different races, and most of the quality scientific argument goes back to whether those differences are heritable or environmental. We'll break down some ways to argue against this book in a moment, but first let's do some math, because math is fun.

Mapping IQ to INT

I'm about to give every statistician in the audience a heart attack, because the shape of the gaussian distribution of IQ does not match the overall shape of the 3d6 bell curve, especially at the tails. But in the end these approximations aren't too terrible for the middle, and I wanted to keep them simple for the muggles. Since we're manipulating median numbers, we'll work with one standard deviation of the mean.

IQ tests are intentionally rigged to have a median of 100, with 68% of the population between 85 and 115. 68% of the Dungeons and Dragons population has an INT between 8 and 13, so let's take that band as roughly approximate. That means around the median, every 6 points of IQ is roughly equivalent to 1 point of INT.

If we're going to translate median racial IQ differences to Dungeons and Dragons INT bonuses, we'd need a table showing median IQ by race. A table like this is very hard to come by, although all serious scientists indicate that there are differences. The best one I could find is from a site called aristocratofthesoul.com, and I cannot vouch for its source because they don't list one, but I have definitely heard some of the numbers there repeated by scientists before.

Based on that table, and our correlative approximations, here are the Gygaxian Earth Race modifiers for INT on a 3d6 ability scale:

- Ashkenazi Jews: +1.7
- East Asians: +0.8

- Europeans: -0.5
- Native Americans: -1.6
- Latin Americans: -1.8
- African Americans: -2.5
- Middle Easterners and North Africans: -2.6
- Sub-Saharan Africans: -5

Now we have some perspective.

The very bad way to argue against Charles Murray is to claim there's no such thing as race (per *Newsweek's* "Why Are We Divided by Race When There Is No Such Thing?"), or to call him a racist for claiming there's a racial bonus to INT (as Southern Poverty Law Center has).

I mean, he might be racist. I don't know, because I've never met the guy. But if someone claims he's racist simply for mentioning something that's verified by numbers, then they automatically undermine their own case and buttress Murray's. Ignoring numbers is a very bad way to win an argument.

The smart, scientific way to argue against *The Bell Curve* is to peel apart what the word "heritable" actually means, in a detailed and deep-thinking way, as Bret Weinstein and Heather Heying do in *The Fifth Column*'s 99th podcast episode published May 1st, 2018. (If you just Googled it, jump forward to the 37-minute mark for the piece most relevant to this essay).

Just looking at the difference in the table above between Sub-Saharan Africans and their United States descendants seems to me to show very plainly that at least a lot of this disparity is environmental in nature. Bret Weinstein in the above podcast makes a compelling case that environmental factors could even show up as heritable in the statistics, owing to lead exposure or nutrition or who knows what else. But, again, I'm not making the position that anything in the book is right or wrong. I'm making the position that very soon nothing in the book will matter anyway because we're about to get a very, very different dungeon master.

Meet the New DM

After about ten gaming sessions you, Joe, and your other friends are deep into your Dungeons and Dragons campaign. Your strength-based character is having a really hard time, because STR is a wallpapered statistic in this game world, while Joe's character has amassed a small fortune selling horseshoes that his newly crafted stone golem pounds out over on the Grayhawk City lower east side. Linda's Bard, a character strong in Charisma, is doing okay playing the bagpipes in dockside taverns, and Larry's Cleric has a pretty good worshiper following of disenfranchised blacksmiths, but neither are remotely keeping pace with the Wizard.

Your old DM gets burned out, and you get a new one you met at Dragon-

Con last year in the dealer's room. She's wearing red horns and is carrying a rattle-wand-thingy.

She takes over one night, identifies the curious plight this game world is experiencing in terms of class imbalance, and has a unique solution. Her first session, the King's cryers announce that a certain courtier, Sir Jawbs, has invented a new magic item,called a "Smart Stone." Everyone can carry one of these things, which are relatively cheap to manufacture, and get an automatic 13 INT score. What's better, every full moon all Smart Stones will upgrade by +1, expanding their capabilities. They can talk to you, solve problems for you, and make your lives easier.

This is great for the Wizards in the short term, because it gives them a new revenue stream. Anyone can make a Smart Stone who has an 18 INT. Then Joe pipes up. "Woah, wait a minute, what happens when the Smart Stones reach 18?"

And the new GM just smiles.

And you smile a bit too.

But the biggest smiles are on the faces of Linda and Larry because nobody's wallpapered their characters yet, while Joe, in a panic, starts yammering on about Universal Basic Platinum and Wizcoin.

Here Be Dragons

When the Silicon Valley intellectual elite foretell the Artificial Intelligence Apocalypse, their doom and gloom is couched as if it's a concern for the wellbeing of mankind. But it seems to me to be disingenuous, or myopic, or both. They're not actually worried about our demise; they're worried about theirs. The intellectuals have already wallpapered the STR jobs, through the industrial revolution, the transition of manufacturing to robots, and the mechanization of agriculture. They already made STR not matter, materially, to success. That INT would be next on the chopping block is not any more a disaster than the last time it happened. What's interesting to me is to think deeply about how the automation process will shift market power to the remaining four ability scores. Charisma in the form of art, Wisdom in the form of spirituality, Dexterity in the form of skilled trades, and Constitution in some form, perhaps the ability to survive the coming antibiotic collapse, may simply become the important remaining character defining statistics.

And nobody cares about Charles Murray anymore, until his granddaughter publishes an updated edition of *The Bell Curve* stating that black people have a heritable edge in jazz music, and then we can all have more handwaving freakoutery.

And what happens to our intrepid Dungeons and Dragons group once every character in Greyhawk has an 18 in every ability score, and there are no more dragons to fight? Well, I guess that group of characters is going to have to open up a gaming shop in Greyhawk, invent an in-character version of Dungeons and Dragons, and start playing it.

And round we go.

Why Are Young Adult Fiction Writers Cannibalizing Each Other?

An appeal for nuance in the age of Cancel Culture

by Marie Eberle

Last year, Amélie Wen Zhao was considered the rising star in the YA literature world. Her success read like a 21st century fairytale: she had participated in a Twitter pitching event for marginalized writers (Zhao immigrated from China to the U.S. at the age of 18) and landed a $500,000 three-book deal with Delacorte Press, a division of Random House. Her debut YA fantasy book, *Blood Heir*, was scheduled for release in summer 2019.

But it all came crashing down in January 2019. A blogger accused Zhao of "gathering screenshots of people who don't/didn't like her book" but stopped short of offering evidence to support this claim. It was enough to spark off a social media hailstorm. Other Twitter users, Goodreads book reviewers who had received advanced reading copies of the book, and even other published authors jumped into the discussion. The attacks launched against Zhao varied wildly: some accused her of plagiarising *Lord of the Rings* by using the line "Don't go where I can't follow"; others claimed the same scene plagiarised *The Hunger Games*. The heaviest charge levied against her is the accusation of antiblack racism.

The latter is the hardest one to assess, especially in the absence of the actual book. Some commenters maintain this claim, while others have softened their criticism, especially since new facts have emerged since the controversy erupted on Twitter.

Zhao's case appears to be part of a pattern: just a few weeks later, the debut novel of one of her most vocal critics, Kosoko Jackson's *A Place For Wolves*, was similarly cancelled by Jackson himself.

What is Cancel Culture?
"Cancelling" people, organisations, or even concepts is a relatively new

phenomenon. In its expression, it is similar to any generic backlash that might occur in the public eye, but its essence feels more tinged with emotions, similar to an angry response to a personal injury.

Lisa Nakamura, Professor at and Director of the Digital Studies Institute at the University of Virginia, studies race and gender in new media, and defines it in the following way:

"It's a cultural boycott. It's an agreement not to amplify, signal boost, give money to. People talk about the attention economy — when you deprive someone of your attention, you're depriving them of a livelihood."

Along similar lines, Meredith Clark, Professor for Media Studies, characterizes cancel culture as the withdrawal of support from someone who was once popular but has committed something so offensive that it warrants the loss of their social status:

"To me, it's ultimately an expression of agency. To a certain extent: I really do think of it like a breakup and a taking back of one's power."

The way Zhao's first book was called off has been widely criticized as a classic case of cancel culture.

However, much of this discussion, particularly articles written by established, white authors, dissolved into point-blank attacks on criticism of racist tropes in general. Wilfully or not, a lot of people misunderstood the original issue and assumed YA Twitter was asking everyone to never ever mention racism in books again.

Just to reiterate this point — the issue was not that Zhao talked about racism. The issue was that large parts of her audience came to the understanding that Zhao, someone who is not black, created a character, who was perceived to be black and killed off at a slave auction, in a world, in which the enslaved part of the population possesses genetic powers that might justify their oppression. In a U.S.-American context, this is a textbook case of perpetuating anti-blackness — the notion that oppression of black people is ubiquitous and justified, and may serve for monetary exploitation by non-black creators. These tropes have historic weight behind them and are easily traced back to the very real oppression black people have faced and continue to face.

The problem here, though, lies in the fact that although it was written and slated for publication in the U.S.A., Zhao didn't write it in an American context. As she explained in her apology letter after pulling it from her publishers:

Here is the issue with this conversation:

Much of the 'cancellation' of both Zhao's and Jackson's books occurred within the YA world. Callouts and consequences occurred swiftly, mainly driven by voices known in the community, but not very widely beyond it. Zhao and Jackson took criticism voiced by their own community to heart and vowed to do better in the future, to general appraisal of their original critics. However, the people reporting on these controversies in bigger literature outlets are almost always outsiders.

They often describe the YA community as a free-speech hating cult killing their own over wokeness points. For example, an article in the *Tablet* called the critics a "social media mob," while a *Slate* article lamented the "evermore-baroque standards for who can write about whom under what circumstances" (the meaning of the word "baroque" in this context beats me). An article in the *Times* went so far as to proclaim the advent of fanatical ideologues: "Purity tests are the tools of fanatics, and the quest for purity ultimately becomes indistinguishable from the quest for power."

The difference between these lit writers and the community they're criticizing could not be starker. The literary publishing world is highly homogenous: according to a 2015 survey by Lee & Low Books, editors are 82 per cent white and less than 2 percent black.

What the *Tablet* articles and many others like it decry as pitchfork-and-torch hysterics is exactly the same kind of work stereotypical in-house editors and book reviewers do; it's just that for once it's voiced by a younger, much more diverse crowd. Most importantly, these Twitter arguments are just that — arguments on social media. When bigger authors and publishers lament censorship in the YA community, all they are talking about are bad Goodreads reviews, Tweets, and some lost revenue the authors were never entitled to in the first place — if people (or the free market-place of ideas, you might say) don't like the book, you have no right to force them to read it, no matter whether it's because they think it's culturally insensitive or just plain bad. In any case, none of that is censorship.

Personally, I can't tell you whether the book should have been cancelled, or whether it would have contributed to negative stereotypes.

Ultimately, the decision lies with the one responsible, that is the author. In Zhao's and Jackson's cases, I applaud them for making a decision not many others would have taken, which was to pull their books.

But what I find unacceptable are critics around the globe complaining about the imagined death of creativity if writers are supposedly not allowed to write outside their own experiences anymore. But that's really not getting it right.

If you actually follow the YA discussions on Twitter, you'll find highly advanced and in-depth critiques of modern race, gender, sexuality, and nationality relations, often delving deeply into territory that'd be worthy of post-graduate level social science. But you would never know that if you just follow the mainstream articles about it, which inevitably describe only the worst of it.

Is there still room for debate about Zhao's and Jackson's cases? Certainly. The topics we should be discussing include the fact that both are writers of color, and Jackson also identifies as queer, who have just taken a serious hit to their careers in an industry that remains disproportionally white, straight, cis, and wealthy, despite repeated claims to change these power imbalances. There is a real danger that risk-averse publishing houses will take the wrong message from this and reverse their decisions to focus more on literature by minorities, afraid of further controversies.

This new generation of YA writers understand themselves to be cultural influencers and educators. They are highly conscious of the weight their words carry, and want to do the very best by their audiences. We are not helping them or their communities if we let people who fundamentally misunderstand the problem dominate the discussions and ruin them with accusations of censorship.

For example, once the cries of censorship by established authors went viral, the YA authors mentioned above had to face an onslaught of harassment. Ellen Oh went so far as to delete her Twitter account completely. What effectively ended up happening was that the followers of people who so vigorously defended free speech in the literary world shut up the voices of some of the most vulnerable and least established writers in the scene.

The questions we should be asking are whether and to what extent should we demand perfection of every piece of representation in a world that is severely lacking of it? If written in good faith, rather than bad faith or ignorance, can we salvage pieces? And then when they are written in good faith but still harmful, how can we teach people to do better while protecting our vulnerable? As Katy Waldman asks in the New Yorker:

And, in my opinion most importantly, how come this cancel culture in the YA community seems to be disproportionately directed at writers who are already part of a marginalized community?

We are not doing anyone a favour if we ignore these questions over accusations of (self-)censorship and social justice ideology gone rogue. More often than not, it's not the YA world and the arguments between authors and their intended audience that lack nuance, but the reports on its infighting. Let's make sure we pay attention to this the next time a young, marginalized YA author appears to fall victim to their own community.

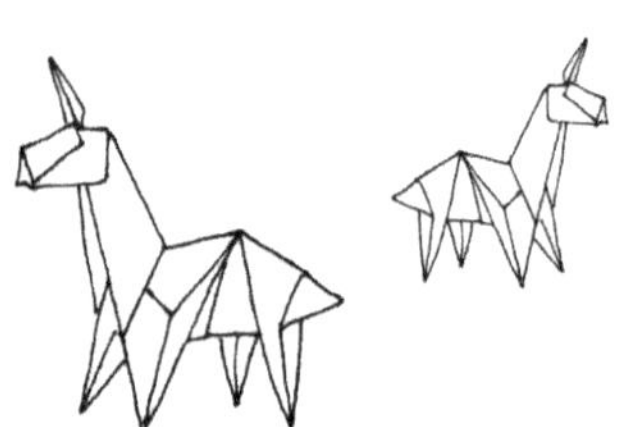

THE IMPORTANCE OF THE ORIGAMI UNICORN

A personal story of loss, friendship, and remembering through *Blade Runner*

by Bill Henning

There's a split in the *Blade Runner* fanworld between people who feel that Deckard is a replicant (bioengineered android), and those who believe he is human. I am firmly on the side that he is human, and no one will ever change my mind on that…unless it's March 14th.

Two years ago a good friend of mine took his own life, and has left a deep hole in my heart when it comes to the subject of the origami unicorn. Joe believed Deckard was a replicant, and we would talk for hours discussing why we thought the other was wrong and why we believed that our version told a better story.

I romanticize the history of these conversations mainly because I don't want to remember them for what they were. Things got heated, both of us getting so angry at each other that we would both just drop the conversation and not say anything, until one of us decided to bring it back up and we restate our stories all over again.

It hurts me that Joe never saw *Blade Runner 2049*. I sometimes wonder what our conversations would have been on the subject, what new arguments we'd have with the sequel. But I'll never know. All I do know is every time I see the unicorn now, the first thing that comes to my mind isn't the question of whether Deckard is human or not. Now it is a symbol of something I have lost and can never have again. It hurts but not in a way I want to shy away from; it is a pain I want to embrace.

Recently I picked up some origami paper and have started to try and fold the unicorn. It isn't easy, and my first attempt turned out to be a total mess. I won't stop though; it is a small promise I made to myself to master making…so I can always take the unicorn with me.

I miss my friend.

To everyone and anyone who ever has the thought of taking their life, please say something. There are people who love you and will listen.

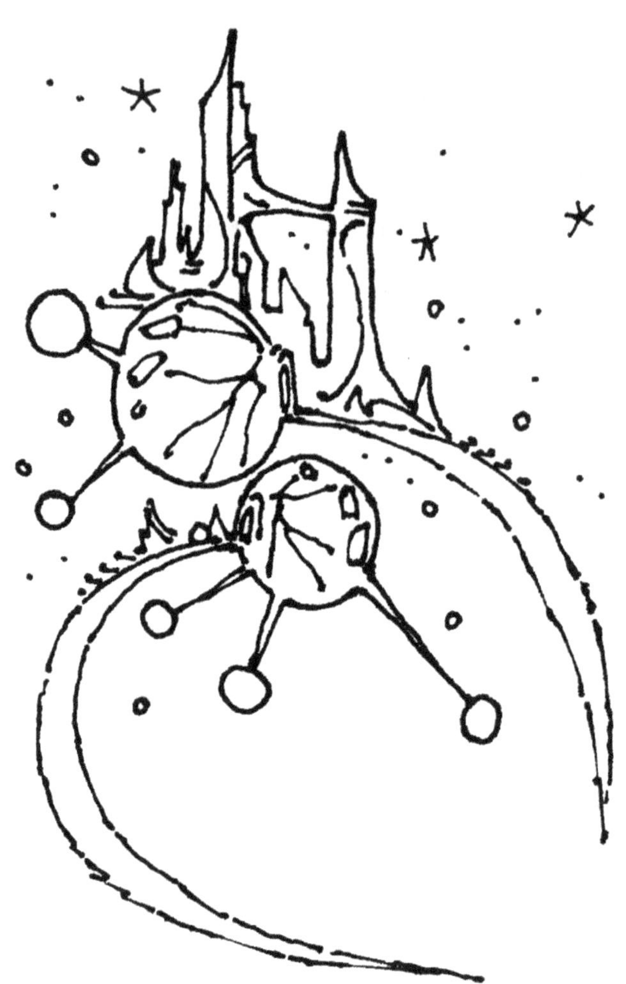

A WORKSHOP ON COSPOETRY
New name; old form

by Marjorie Steele

I recently ran a writing workshop for a local arts organization, during which we played with a form I've dubbed cospoetry.

This is also, as you may notice, a category I use on this publication. It occurred to me during the workshop that I've never bothered really defining what I mean by "cospoetry" here, nor — more importantly — why I think it's a poetic form that deserves our attention as readers.

Also, my workshop attendees seemed to really enjoy themselves, and they created some really fascinating work during the workshop. So I'm sharing with you what I shared with them.

While we can't really recreate an in-person workshop in this setting, I do encourage you to try a hand at writing your own cospoem — and, of course, submitting it for publication here.

So, what exactly IS cospoetry?

To my knowledge, I *think* I may have invented this phrase, as it relates to poetry, but the poetic form I'm identifying as "cospoetry" is far from novel. In fact, in a way, it's been used by poets for millennia.

Cospoetry is, as I define it:

A POEM WHICH USES ELEMENTS, THE LENS, OR CHARACTERS AND MYTHOLOGIES FROM KNOWN SCIENCE FICTION OR FANTASY STORIES AND PRINCIPLES IN ORDER TO ILLUMINATE A UNIVERSAL TRUTH WHICH TRANSCENDS TIME, SPACE, AND CULTURE.

In this way, it's not meter, rhyme, or stanza count which defines the form — as is the case with structure-based forms like sonnets, odes, and the like — but the thematic elements which the poem uses to create meaning.

These poems connect with readers through the common vernacular of sci-fi and fantasy stories and concepts, allowing those fluent to experience intimate familiarity with the subject matter, while also transporting readers to another time/place.

What's new about that?

Absolutely nothing; poets have been telling stories about stories, and mixing science and myth with real life experience for millennia.

The only thing that's really new, to be honest, is my own perspective on writing work that's referential. While I was in college (majoring in creative writing/poetry), I surmised, based on the works around me and the general "rules" of poetry I observed, that writing works which are referential to the themes, characters, and worlds of other works was Right Out.

I've always had this itch to write a poetry chapbook about the Avengers: a sonnet for Thor, a sestina for Tony Stark, and of course, an e.e.cummings style nonsensical free form for Hulk. But pop culture references are problematic because then the work relies on the audience's knowledge of the work you're referencing, which means it can't stand on its own, blah blah blah.

But what I've realized, lately, is that's all just silly. Those are silly and arbitrary barriers. Poets have been referencing other stories, and using the devices that others have established, since literally the dawn of human consciousness.

Much of modern poetry is riddled with Greek mythology and art history references (W.C. Williams' *Pictures from Brueghel*, I'm looking at you); this is seen as "high art," and so (I surmise) generally more accepted in the academic community, but here's the thing:

I don't want to write about Greek tragedies. I want to write about Carol Danvers. And Carrie Fisher. And also the 5th dimension, and the meaning of Life as it's written in the stars.

Cospoetry throughout history

As it turns out, I'm in very good company.

Once you begin to look, history is littered with cospoetry — at least, what I've identified as such.

Drawing from the folklore side of fantasy, pulitzer-prize winning modernist poet Anne Sexon sparked a trend in the "anti-grotesque" with her scathingly sarcastic retelling of "Cinderella" in 1971:

CINDERELLA AND THE PRINCE
LIVED, THEY SAY, HAPPILY EVER AFTER,
LIKE TWO DOLLS IN A MUSEUM CASE
NEVER BOTHERED BY DIAPERS OR DUST,
NEVER ARGUING OVER THE TIMING OF AN EGG,

80 years earlier, poet and Irish nationalist William Yeats was writing about his favorite characters from the pantheon of Irish mythology: Fergus mac Róich, Cuchulain, the Red Branch Warriors, and the Kingdom of Ulster. In "Who goes with Fergus?" Yeats is referencing a point of the story when Fergus is banished from his kingdom after being shamefully tricked out of his rightful kingship by the raping and pillaging Conchobar mac Nessa:

WHO WILL GO DRIVE WITH FERGUS NOW,
AND PIERCE THE DEEP WOOD'S WOVEN SHADE,
AND DANCE UPON THE LEVEL SHORE:
YOUNG MAN, LIFT UP YOUR RUSSET BROW,
AND LIFT YOUR TENDER EYELIDS, MAID,
AND BROOD ON HOPES AND FEAR NO MORE.
AND NO MORE TURN ASIDE AND BROOD
UPON LOVE'S BITTER MYSTERY;
FOR FERGUS RULES THE BRAZEN CARS,
AND RULES THE SHADOWS OF THE WOOD,
AND THE WHITE BREAST OF THE DIM SEA
AND ALL DISHEVELLED WANDERING STARS.

Oh man, that last line always gets me.

We can keep tracing this back.

The oldest recorded Welsh poet, Taleisin, known in older Arthurian legends (i.e. original Welsh stories, before the Francization of the story after the Norman conquest) as the Bard of King Arthur, himself draws on more ancient stories and both mythological and mystical references, in his poem "Battle of Trees":

FROM THE ESSENCE OF SOIL WAS I MADE,
FROM THE BLOOM OF NETTLES, FROM WATER OF THE NINTH WAVE.
MATH ENCHANTED ME BEFORE I WAS MOBILE;
GWYDION CREATED ME, GREAT MAGIC FROM THE STAFF OF ENCHANT-
MENT;
FROM EURWYS AND EURON, FROM EURON AND MODRON,
FROM FIVE FIFTIES OF MAGICIANS AND TEACHERS LIKE MATH WAS I
PRODUCED.
THE LORD PRODUCED ME WHEN HE WAS QUITE INFLAMED;
THE MAGICIAN OF MAGICIANS CREATED ME BEFORE THE WORLD —
WHEN I HAD EXISTENCE, THERE WAS EXPANSE TO THE WORLD.
FAIR BARD! OUR CUSTOM IS PROFIT; I CAN PUT IN SONG WHAT THE
TONGUE CAN UTTER...[EXCERPT]

This is from the 14th century manuscript the *Book of Taleisin*, although due to the nature of how oral history was typically recorded, we can safely assume this work is at least several hundred years older -- quite possibly as far back as 550 A.D., which is when some historians speculate the King Arthur story originated.

It keeps going. We can go all the way back to one of the most ancient, most complete poetic narratives we have from human history: Gilgamesh. This ancient verse, which dates back to 3,000 B.C. (or further — again, due to the nature of oral history), is riddled with cultural references. Names of forests and cities, mythical guardians, gods and goddesses, and so on.

The Epic of Gilgamesh is set in a foreign landscape, riddled with alien supernatural figures, yet its universal human truths shine like a spotlight across more than five millennia. It's one of the most stunning examples of the synchronicity of the common elements of storytelling we have. And it's heavily referential to the works and cultural references of another time and place.

All these works — and so many others — are referential.

So let's ask ourselves: if you as the reader don't know the context of the story they reference, do these works still succeed — at least, on some level?

Yes.

Does knowing the backstory of the reference — i.e., sharing a tie of kinship with the author — enhance and enrich the work?

Absofuckinglutely.

That's all you can really ask from a successful poem, isn't it? To stand on its own well enough, and to have more depth to yield based on its relevance to the reader?

Modern cospoetry

Cospoetry is actually everywhere — once you start to look for it.

A favorite Medium fiction writer of mine, Evan Fleischer, wrote in his breathless little piece, "Space.", published in issue #1 of this series.

THE ONLY BIT OF LANGUAGE WE'VE BEEN ABLE TO DECODE FROM IT SO FAR IS "STARS," SIR. STARS? THAT'S ALL IT'S SAYING: "STARS. STARS, STARS, STARS. STARS." [EXCERPT]

I almost die, every time I read that. There's just something about it.

Why? Because I consume a steady diet of science fiction, science neat, and general space-and-time related shenaniganery on a daily basis, because I fucking love that shit. So when you tell me there's an alien lifeform that's taken over a ship and wants to be fed poetry and its only decipherable communication is a morse code of the word "stars," my response is: FUCK YES, MOAR PLEASE.

Would you like Evan's poem if you don't love sci-fi? I dunno, maybe? Does it matter? No. Of course it doesn't.

I actually wrote what would qualify as a cospoem last spring, which won a local poetry award, before I'd coined the term.

The sci-fi elements come out most strongly in the title and the epitaph, which are both quotes from one of my favorite shows, *Battlestar Galactica* (the new one, by Ronald D. Moore).

Which provides a strong contrast to the subject matter, which is actually about an Irish ancestor from the late 1700s. I do get a little referential towards the end of the poem, although instead of tying it back to the future with sci-fi, I connect it to an even further past with a fantasy/mythology reference:

WHAT SEEDS DID SHE CARRY WITH HER TO THE NEW WORLD?
RESIGNATION IS NOWHERE FOUND WITHIN MY FAMILY LINE,
AND BY THAT I MEAN NOT THE LINE OF CUCHULAIN, OF BUDDICA, OF
THE
FIERCE WESTERN ISLES
BUT THE LINE OF EVE.

My old poetry prof, Oliver de la Paz (who by synchronicity was also the judge of the poetry competition this poem anonymously won), seemed to dig the sci-fi overtones.

Which, in retrospect, is not that surprising, because it's a technique which has also been recently used by a colleague of his, and a far more authoritative poet than me: our new US Poet Laureate, Tracy K. Smith herself, in her latest chapbook: *Life On Mars*.

Last fall, I had the privilege of seeing both Tracy and Oliver read their work at a local college arts festival, and I was both enraptured by Tracy's work, and felt vindicated by its subject matter.

As she read her opening poem, "My God, It's Full of Stars," and eulogized on about Stanley Kubrick's classic 1968 movie 2001 Space Odyssey, actor names and all, all I could think was:

Shit, you mean that's allowed???

She even opens the chapbook with a poem titled "Sci-Fi:"

Tracy's take, unlike a lot of the doom-and-gloom sentiment we get from classical sci-fi canon like Azimov, Herbert, and the inventor of the genre, Mary Shelley herself, is quite optimistic. It's rather more in line with Gene Roddenberry's Trekkian vision of a future filled with peace and unity—but grounded in the modern and familiar, as in her villanelle "Solstice":

I really like the way Tracy uses sci-fi throughout the book: not as an escape, but quite the opposite. She uses it to connect, as an avenue to express a vested interest in examining what's wrong with what humanity is doing, with a positive outlook towards our progression — whatever form that takes. It assumes the inevitability of life, and embraces the cycle of creation and destruction, with a drive to become incrementally more perfect, more whole, as individuals and as a network of life-forms, and to achieve something which is greater than the sum of our parts.

I like that idea a lot. And cospoetry, by its nature, lends itself to that optimistic exploration really, really well.

Digging deep: source materials & further reading

As I told my workshop attendees, rather than riddling you with a plethora of further examples, I want to leave you with a small handful of what we could call "primary sources" instead.

Based on my research, I believe these primary sources lead us towards many of the key principles which sci-fi and fantasy express so well, which are so integral to the experience of being human: exploration, interconnection, unity, balance, wholeness.

"THE EMERALD TABLETS" OF THOTH-THE-ATLANTE-AN

Oh yes. I told you we were digging deep.

Allegedly authored by the Atlantean Priest-King Thoth, who came to Egypt as a lone refugee, the Emerald Tablets are discarded by the mainstream scientific community as folklore of unknowable origins. Yet this work has been translated by some of history's most celebrated scientific minds, including Sir Isaac Newton (a portion of his translation is currently on display at Cambridge University).

We call them scientists, but Newton and his contemporaries considered themselves avid alchemists, and were prolific scholars of astrology and Hermetic philosophy, which originated in ancient Greece and Egypt.
Which brings us to:

"The Divine Pymander" by Hermes Trismegistus

Allegedly the account of scribe of the gods of ancient Egypt: Hermes Trismegistus, *Corpus Hermeticium: The Divine Pymander* is the foundational source material for Hermeticism. The echoes of Hermeticism can be traced back before Plato, who himself passed along stories of lost Atlantis, as well as Hermetic philosophy, as told to him by an Egyptian priest.

Iterations of the themes Thoth and Hermes write about inform the nature of the Universe, the relationship between good and evil, the interconnectivity between all living things, the role of the planets and the stars, and our proximity to alternate dimensions — or levels of consciousness, if you will. These themes can be seen being played out in religions like Christianity, Islam, and Zoroastrianism; in literature and philosophy from east and west, and — most especially—in science fiction and fantasy; and in the ancient practice of alchemy, upon which modern scientific practice is based.

Thoth and Hermes' students over the millennia have included Plutarch, Newton, Marquis de Sade, Arthur Conan Doyle, *Star Trek* creator Gene Roddenberry, and I'm sure a host of women whose name didn't make it to the lists, because, well…we've gotten overlooked quite a bit since Thoth was in his glory days.

"Real Alchemy: A Primer of Practical Alchemy"

This applies hermetic principles in very concrete ways to the world around us, and alchemy is, as we were taught in school, the pursuit of turning lead into gold, but in a metaphorical way — not the asininely literal interpretation which is typically applied. It's about catalyzing things to achieve their purest form.
Alchemy is scientific in its approach, but unlike modern science, it incorporates metaphysical elements, rather than ignoring them.

Which leads me to my last referral:

REVIEWS

DUNE.

Why We Need Another 'Dune' Movie

An essential tale for modern times comes back to the big screen

by Richard Brownell

If you are a true fan of a particular piece of art, then you never have to make an apology for it. Love means never having to say you're sorry — right?

Whether it's a certain book, a movie, or whatever, we all possess a guilty pleasure for something that a larger segment of the population either disregards, misunderstands, or looks down on as ephemeral or even low-rent. So it has been with *Dune*.

Don't get me wrong. Frank Herbert's original 1965 novel is a seminal work for the serious sci-fi afficianado. In the fifty-plus years since its publication, the book has received awards and accolades, and even mainstream acceptance as one of the great novels of the 20th century. Some of that wider critical recognition has come with clenched teeth, but science fiction has always had a tough time being taken as serious art (whatever that's supposed to be).

Dune has earned every bit of praise it has received over the years. Herbert spent five years working on the book. He managed to get it serialized in a magazine, but no book publisher would touch it. Too long, too convoluted, not interesting, dryly written, there were all sorts of excuses. The one publisher brave enough to take on the first printing, Chilton Books, was a company that published auto repair manuals and had zero experience or market share in fiction.

Dune was the little engine that could of science fiction. It found an audience in hardcore sci-fi fans that slowly but steadily grew over the years. Several sequels followed, and even some erstwhile film adaptations, but despite it all, *Dune* never garnered the widespread crossover appeal of fantasy franchises like *Star Wars*, *Harry Potter*, *Lord of the Rings*, *Marvel*, or *Star Trek*.

The big reason for this may be that *Dune* is heavier than what would normally pass for mass-market sci-fi. Without even going into the full Duniverse (I love that term!), just the first book alone is a lot to tackle.

The original *Dune* is not a breezy read. I tried to crack it when I was a kid, and the book kicked my ass. It wasn't until I was 20 and hip deep in a poli-sci program at a run-of-the-mill liberal arts college that I finally absorbed and fell in love with it. Please note that it doesn't take a trip through college studying a major free of career opportunities and smoking good weed to comprehend *Dune*. I've read it a couple times since without all that, and I still dig it.

Dune has a lot of layers to it. Herbert takes on ecology and environment, religion and faith, politics and palace intrigue, labor and economics, immigration and minority rights. Seriously: this book has it all. I won't go too far into the details of the plot except to say it involves an attempt to take control of a planet pivotal to the economic and intellectual life of the known universe in the year 10,191.

Dune is an epic saga with a great cast of characters, but it doesn't contain any of the trappings that easily translate into big screen success. It doesn't have any cuddly creatures; it has sandworms that are several hundred feet long. It doesn't have sharp-tongued sidekicks; it has Mentats — human computers with no personality. It doesn't have exotic locations full of color and beauty; it has a northern desert, a southern desert, and a great wall of rock that separates the two.
It could be *Dune's* utter lack of mass-market tropes that has made it such a difficult story to convert to film. Avant-garde filmmaker Alejandro Jodorowsky tried to put together an adaptation that would have included the talents of Salvador Dali, Orson Welles, Mick Jagger, H.R. Giger, Moebius, and Pink Floyd. But that was in the pre-*Star Wars* days, and no studio would touch it.

David Lynch famously tackled the book in 1984, and despite the film's generally poor reviews and box office, and Lynch's own disavowal of the movie, it has managed to earn a cult following over the years. The Sci-Fi Channel, before it became SyFy, adapted *Dune* as a miniseries in 2000 and did quite well with it. It remains to this day one of their highest rated original programs.

Still, *Dune* deserves another chance at the big screen, and it looks like it will finally be getting it. Just recently it was announced that Denis Villeneuve will be helming at two-part film adaptation of the original book. He has the blessing of Brian Herbert, Frank's son and co-author of the ongoing Dune-iverse books, and the support of Legendary Entertainment, the latest film studio to hold the rights to the *Dune* property.

Villeneuve refers to *Dune* as *Star Wars* for adults. He's right. In fact, you can see a lot of *Dune* in George Lucas's original 1977 film. Villeneuve is also right when he says that *Dune* will be a challenge.

Adapting *Dune* wouldn't be worthwhile if it wasn't a challenge. But I am confident that this new version will deliver the goods. First, Villeneuve is a filmmaker with a true appreciation for visual storytelling. I was very skeptical about a *Blade Runner* reboot from the start, but when I sat down in the theater to see his *Blade Runner 2049*, I did not want the movie to end. It was amazing on every level. The same can be said for *Arrival*.

Second, now is the perfect time for the story of *Dune* to be redone in a new way on the big screen. So many of the original book's themes are on display in our world right now.

· Ecology and environment — Does man have the right to remake his world today for his own sake, and what is his responsibility to future generations?
· Politics — To what extent are we beholden to the leaders we appoint, and when do we have the right to walk away from the system we created?
· Economics — Every system has the exploited and the exploiters. Who gets to decide who benefits?
· Labor — Who should control the means of production? Those who build the system, or those who work it?

For a story written over 50 years ago, which takes place thousands of years in the future, *Dune* could almost be inspired by today's headlines. Science fiction has always been a great vehicle for examining the human condition. By removing the overtly controversial and replacing it with the allegorical, sci-fi writers have been able to force us to take a good look at ourselves in a way that inspires critical thinking without our built-in prejudices getting in the way.

Dune has that potential. And Denis Villeneuve should be given whatever budget he needs to make the story come to life in a way that entertains, inspires, and makes us think. The time has come.

'Stories Untold': It's All Your Fault
My Favorite Game of 2017

by Bill Henning

2017 had a lot of ups and downs in the video game world. What with the amazing year Nintendo had with the Switch and the catastrophic launch that EA made with *Star Wars Battlefront 2*, it's easy to miss a couple of games here and there. While the indie game market had really taken off, some titles slip through the cracks without anyone noticing. And while I put hundreds of hours into games like *Injustice 2*, *Play Unknown Battle-grounds*, and *Horizon Zero Dawn*, my favorite game of the year was only three hours long but had one of the best and favorite gaming moments of my life: *Stories Untold*.

Nostalgia Warning

Stories Untold is a nostalgia trip, riding the feelings of '80s science fiction and horror. It feels like it was ripped from an unpublished Stephen King novel, and it's quite proud of it. The opening theme is a call back to the '80s that most people today will say reminds them of *Stranger Things*. That is a great way to set you up to play a dread-filled, text-based adventure, puzzle, horror game.

Wait, wait, wait, wait! Don't judge this game by its being a text-based adventure game! You might find yourself asking how this game can be a horror game if it is just writing answers into a computer. Well, that's part of the beauty of this game, which I'll explain, being very careful about spoilers.

Stories Untold is broken up into four episodes, each dealing with a different style of puzzle mechanic and each having its own enclosed story. One deals with a haunted house, another an alien invasion, and so on. Each feels like an episode you'd see from *The Twilight Zone* or *The Outer Limits*; each one feels self-contained. But as each story unfolds, you start to see that they're all connected. Even knowing what all of the episodes mean and how they connect wouldn't spoil the game, but again the less you know, the more fun you'll have. Let's just say that after I finished the final episode, I went back and replayed the first three just to see how much they were connected.

That's the strongest point of the game: every part of the game can be peeled away like an onion to show layers and layers of depth. My friend played the first episode demo and explored every part of the house and simply asked me why he couldn't make it into the cellar, something I didn't question while I played it as I just figured it was a part of the haunted house not implemented into the game. The next day when I finished the final episode I texted him back in all capitals; "THERE IS A REASON!"

The demo is free and lets you play the first level, "The House Abandon." This episode is less puzzle based and more of the straightforward text-based adventure game as you find yourself sitting at a desk with an old gaming system sitting in front of you. It's only about twenty minutes long, but it's responsible for this being my game of the year. As the plot unfolds, and the twist comes, you become so unhinged and filled with fear that you want to stop playing, but you can't.

...This Was All...

Stories Untold doesn't hold your hand, and it leaves very few hints for you to figure out some of its more complicated puzzles. This is the only real downside to the game: as text-based games often are, it is very unforgiving when it comes to word usage.

Episodes two and three are much more puzzle based. Each episode deals with multiple screens — usually one with the puzzle and one with the answers needed to solve it. The puzzles become more and more elaborate, until they make a larger logic jump than I was expecting.

Episode two suffers from its jumping halfway through back into the text-based adventure game, which I found very jarring. It's helped by the story, as it becomes more and more creepy. Episode three, on the other hand, suffers completely from the story falling apart, with the setup being very interesting as it progresses but ultimately fails at delivering in both story and payoff. While both of these bothered me, the final episode fixes it all.

...Your Fault...

Stories Untold's style and gameplay make it stand out against every other game I played this year. The story that unfolds is unique and tells an unsettling and intriguing story. The music hits you with the right amount of nostalgia, without feeling forced. While I did have problems toward the middle and end of the story, how everything is told and connected at the end more than made up for this fault. This game is a prime example of how video games can tell a narrative that books or movies can't, how video games can be the truly interactive experience, and this is why it's my game of 2017.

Just remember...it was all your fault.

'JOJO RABBIT'S' SATIRICAL DANCE OF DESTRUCTION

Taika Waititi vaults over Wes Anderson's head in his Hindu-esque dance of comedy and death

by Marjorie Steele

It's not very often you say to your family, "hey, there's a new movie out about a young Nazi kid in WWII whose imaginary friend is Hitler. I hear it's hilarious. Let's go see it."

As film star Scarlett Johansson and writer, director, and co-star Taika Waititi have both pointed out: the film's log line doesn't read well. At all. But, appropriately in step with the lessons our young hero learns in the film itself, public perception isn't always truth. In fact, oftentimes, it's quite the opposite.

Aside from the unanimously pitch-perfect performances, a brilliant script, meticulous directing, gorgeous cinematography, a searingly appropriate soundtrack, and just about every other technical aspect you could mention, this movie is also just plain genius. It's a brilliant shining gem of human empathy and emotional ingenuity. It made me belly laugh. It made me shout. It made me gasp. It made me grab my daughter and cover her eyes as I sobbed, being suddenly reminded how pivotal and fleeting my role as mother is — and that each joyful moment is precious.

I love Wes Anderson and his work dearly. But I think it may be time for him to retire. In *JoJo Rabbit*, Taika has taken so many of the highly stylized techniques we're used to seeing in an Anderson film — fast-paced and witty dialogue, extremely specific costuming and set design, action scenes underlined by thematically selected pop music, and a general sense of meticulously curated whimsy — but he's remixed them in a way which is wilder, darker, and sharper. And, quite frankly: while very similar in presentation, the dark and terrifying themes of Waititi's film are very different from Anderson's plots, which tend to revolve around the internal struggles of privileged people. Waititi's themes (see also: *Thor: Ragnarok*) focus on outright colonialization and war.

The theme of trying to to survive Nazi Germany with your morality intact naturally lends itself to a little more societal depth than the theme of trying to survive being adopted into a rich family and falling in love

with your brother (love you forever, Royal Tennenbaums, but you're definite-
ly on about #whitepeopleproblems).

Which is why the Nazi Germany genre is typically reserved for the austere
arthouse film community, in films like *Schindler's List* and *The Piano*, in which
there is much crying and zero laughing.

Not since Roberto Benigni — that tiny little genius madman of an Italian
comedian (and his unaccountably beautiful wife) — made *Life is Beautiful* in
the '90s has anyone been crazy enough to attempt to carve a comedy out of
the events of Nazi Germany. Quentin Tarantino came damned close in 2009
with *Inglorious Bastards*, which was set in a fictional victorious Nazi Germa-
ny, and got roundly slapped by critics for doing so. Regardless, no one to
date, that I'm aware of, has tried to make a Nazi Germany comedy as told
through the eyes of a Nazi child.

But, like Benigni and Tarantino, I don't think anyone would accuse Taika of
being entirely sane. This film is not the creation nor undertaking of a sane
person. But it is clearly the undertaking of a genius. And it seems to me that
Taika's style of crazy is exactly the antidote society needs right now.

After all, as Benigni said in defense of his film:

"TO LAUGH AND CRY COMES FROM THE SAME POINT OF THE SOUL, NO?"

Imaginary friend Adolf: the gut punchingly friendly face of propaganda

It's a tough film to bill because the main premise itself is both scathingly
pointed and bullishly forward. Our main protagonist, 10-year-old Jojo, is
a young German boy living in Nazi Germany who has, like all his peers,
swallowed the propaganda of the Nazi state hook, line, and sinker. To the
extent that his imaginary friend is Adolf Hitler. Except, of course, it's NOT
Adolf Hitler — it's a 10-year-old good-hearted boy's conjuration, which is
an amalgamation of his subconscious and what it's been fed by the society
around him.

Imaginary friend Adolf is played by none other than Taika himself, who
reluctantly places himself in the role of "that idiot," as he refers to his char-
acter in press tours. And Taika's portrayal is every bit as ridiculous as you
would expect it to be — especially when his German accent slips, which is
quite often. And while he does encourage and play as aide to our protagonist
Jojo, Adolf also proves himself to be rather gutless, suspicious, petty, and
vindictive, as far as imaginary friends go.

Out of the gates, the film is forcing us to reimagine the concept of "Hitler"
through the lens of a young innocent who's been the subject to propaganda.
It forces us to empathize with a type of character which is…uncomfortable

for us, on so many levels — but which is also critical for us, in this era of widespread state and corporation-sponsored propaganda.

As a German Nazi espousing Nazi ideals, Jojo would normally be considered a villain. But he's a child — and an innocent, gentle-hearted one at that. In the first act, we see that Jojo doesn't have the heart to pass the older Nazi boys' test of killing a rabbit with his bare hands (hence his nickname, Jojo Rabbit). And he's been fed lies by the authority figures and media around him. So we can't NOT empathize with Jojo on the grounds of his innocence and circumstances because, in many ways, we are Jojo. We are trying to find our own sense of morality and humanity in the midst of a shitstorm of propaganda.

But empathizing with Jojo — a Nazi, even if he is only 10 years old — puts us on very uncomfortable social ground, indeed. Which, again, seems only appropriate for our current political climate of extremism. Who among us has the precognition to say which of our extremist political sects is poised to become the next Nazi party? (Richard Brody over at *The New Yorker* believes that he is, apparently, having criticized this film solely on the basis that he thinks it encourages empathy towards Trump supporters, which is apparently unacceptable under any terms. Which makes me conclude that Brody doesn't understand the film's messages about the nature of propaganda and bigotry — nor does he grasp the concept of nonviolence in general.)

It's worth noting, as Taika himself has cited as being part of his research during the film's press tour, that children in Nazi Germany were directly encouraged by their teachers and authority figures to rebel against their parents, and even to report their parents to the authorities for having anti-Nazi sympathies. The required schooling of Nazi Germany may not have been nearly as cartoonish as it's depicted in *Jojo Rabbit*, but it wasn't far off in terms of content.

We see the impact of this propaganda also play out in the book Jojo is writing about Jews, which is both wildly creative and fantastically inaccurate. He attributes them with horns, telepathy, scales, and all sorts of fantastic supernatural powers, much to the delight and encouragement of the authority figures around him. He presents these findings, and follow-up questions, to Elsa, the Jewish girl his mother is hiding in their house, with comedic audacity. Her response to play along with Jojo's fantastical assertions seems only fitting.
Because, in the face of such propaganda-fed absurdity, what else is there to do but to laugh? The whole thing might be horrific — but it's also just plain silly. And what's the best way to set a bully back on their heels? Laugh in their face.

It successfully jolts Jojo into realizing how ridiculous the propaganda is which he's been sold. Which, in turn, jolts us into realizing how susceptible we as a society are to the endless barrage of hate propaganda around us as well, whether it's spoken by Sean Hannity on Fox News or by Richard Brody at The New Yorker.

On living while mothering, and teaching your child to dance

I can't say that I've ever encountered a mother character in a film quite like Jojo's mother, Rosie (played by Scarlett Johansson). Specifically in the ease of her sense of purpose, her natural comedic quirkiness, and her intimately playful parenting style. She feels more like any other character I've encountered to be a woman who has a life to live, who has a defined sense of personhood, and who in addition to these things is also a mother. And a damned good one at that. Being the mother of a 10-year-old Nazi while harboring a Jewish girl in your house and actively promoting the resistance in the heart of Nazi territory is a razor sharp tightrope to walk. But Rosie does it with a grin and a lightness of foot — with the help of the occasional bottle of wine.

How do you teach your son not to hate when doing so could endanger your very life?

You smear fireplace ash over your chin in lieu of a beard and channel your husband when your son demands to talk to his father. And you give him a realistic act — alcoholism and PTSD-induced verbal abuse included.

You prank him by tying his shoelaces together to remind him that he needs to learn to tie his shoes himself. You volley back his comment that "love is stupid" by replying "you're stupid." You tease him, and play with him, like he's a boy of flesh and bone and not a china doll.

You teach him to dance, and to celebrate life. To nourish his childhood, and to cherish each beautiful moment as a gift, because this is the true value in life — not politics and war games.

You make him look at the dead bodies of the people who were hanged for doing, in Rosie's words, "what they could." You prepare him for your possible demise, in the process.

I'll be honest with you: it was a bit terrifying for me to watch, as I saw some of my own proclivities as a mother so strongly mirrored in Rosie. Even in the theater, I was doing something not dissimilar — drawing my daughter's attention to things which are true. "How did everything get destroyed?" she asks when a scene cuts to the city's bombed-out state. "Planes dropped bombs to try to defeat the Nazis so they stop killing people. And now everyone's home is destroyed. This is what real war looks like. This is what real war does to real people. This happens in real life when people make war." "Yes, I know," she says, this not being her first lecture on the nature of war.

I'm going to hide behind a no spoilers rule on this post and stop my commentary on Rosie there. But, really, the truth is that I just don't have the heart to say more. It's too close to home.

I will say that this is, hands down, the best performance I've seen Scarlett give — and I held her work in quite high regard prior to this film. I really hope Scarlett and Taika do more work together in the future, as Taika clearly has a knack for creating roles which make her comedic and dramatic talents shine, and vice versa.

Captain K: sometimes heroes are also war criminals because people are complicated

Another shining bright star in this movie is Captain K — played to perfection by Sam Rockwell rocking the hell out of a very accurate German accent. As a one-eyed German Nazi war veteran (read: a Nazi war criminal), Captain K's injuries have banished him from the front lines, so he's stuck running war training camp for German kids. He's a cartoonishly outlandish character, and sardonically aware of Nazi Germany's impending doom (and therefore his own), as only Sam Rockwell can pull off.

Captain K has sketched out, in colored pencil, a rendering of his ideal uniform for riding into final battle — resplendent with flowing crimson robes, eyeliner, and a portable record player for blasting music while he charges forward. As Captain K shares this rendering with Jojo, like two children poring over a comic book, Jojo slyly steals some of his coloring pencils, revealing the reality that this rendering is the work of a child in a man's body.

Which, of course, reminds us that the entire Nazi regime is built around one big silly boy's club, all meant to prop up childishly inflated egos. This is something which Elsa, the Jewish girl being hidden by Jojo's mother in their home, reminds Jojo of quite directly:

"YOU'RE NOT A NAZI, JOJO. YOU'RE A 10-YEAR-OLD KID WHO LIKES DRESSING UP IN A FUNNY UNIFORM AND WANTS TO BE PART OF A CLUB."

Jojo is under Captain K's ward when he blows himself up with a grenade in the opening act — a fact which Rosie points out by wordlessly kicking Captain K in the balls and slapping him with her leather glove. The Captain accepts his punishment and ensuing demotion doggedly, and goes about his cartoonishly pointless existence as he waits for the war to end — badly for him and his compatriots.

But, as any great Falstaffian foil does, Captain K offers us more than just comic relief. He is a complex character with a relatable history, and he is not, in the end, without a sense of morality. It's Captain K who arrives just in the nick of time to save Jojo and Elsa from the Gestapo, deftly enough that Jojo and Elsa aren't even sure that Captain K is an ally. And it's Captain K who saves Jojo from the American firing squad in the end. Fittingly, he does this by putting back on his silly Nazi bigotry. But not before Captain K and Jojo share an intimate moment of friendship.

And not before Captain K gets in his glorious last stand, resplendent in his regal uniform and accompanying phonograph sound track. A doomed war criminal, aware that he's hitched himself to the losing party, having no moral allegiance to the cause he's fighting for. Captain K is nothing but a remnant of glory which never was and never will be, and he knows it — yet he chooses to go down in style, according to his own particular idiom. It is not, in many ways, dissimilar to the lesson Rosie was teaching Jojo: to dance, and to celebrate life as the gift it is in each moment, before it slips away.

It's complicated. Because he's a Nazi war criminal, which very likely makes him an outright murderer. And he's also a secret ally to the Jews — or, at least one which we're aware of. He's a self-centered buffoon. But he's also self-aware, and refuses to relinquish his enthusiasm for life, despite the shitty circumstances around him and the shitty decisions which lay behind him.

Captain K is more like the mentors we encounter in real life: complicated, and a mix of good and bad which we have to sort out for ourselves.

Stephen Merchant Gestapo, clones, unicorn for dinner, German shepherd puns, and the Hinduism of dancing

In true gallows humor form, the film's most terrifying character is played by the absurdly funny and physically awkward comedian Stephen Merchant. The balance in Merchant's depiction of this Gestapo leader between hilarity and horror is razor sharp, and makes for one of the most intensely emotional scenes I've encountered. Without saying too much, let's just say that death hangs heavy over this scene and this portion of the film, as does the potential for life. Merchant's portrayal serves to underline the absurdity of the ideology which is driving the horrors at play here. We can't stop laughing, even though we're on the edges of our seats in horror.

Taika's attitude towards life and death shows its colors in moments like these, and reveals itself to be less western in its philosophy, and more eastern. There's a lot of Hindu philosophy at play, here, in my estimation.

We see it in the dark, unflinching whimsy and laugh-out-loud antics
which fill the moments between the plot like mortar between bricks.
The face of Jojo's best friend comedically shrieking over him after Jojo
blows himself up with a grenade. Captain K's doomed and glorious last
stand, and swift end. The rapid and off-handed reference to the swarm
of identical clone boys created by German scientists, who we see again
as they charge the Americans to their deaths. Rebel Wilson's Fraulein
Rahm haphazardly waving and pointing her loaded pistol in everyone's
faces, slapping conscriptions and guns into the hands of children, horrifi-
cally hilarious in her apathy towards human life — including her own. "I
myself have had eighteen children for Germany," she proclaims sardoni-
cally to the children. "It's a vonderful time to be a girl in Germany."

Imaginary friend Adolf dining on a unicorn's head while Jojo rummages
in the trash for his and Elsa's dinner. Captain K's assistant bringing in a
group of old sheep herding conscripts who are Germans, instead of the
dogs the Captain had meant to request — a flat out groaner pun in the
middle of death and destruction.

"It's okay," we hear Captain K comfort his assistant as we pan away, "it's
a shtupid name for a dog, anyvay."

Everywhere, we have death and life smashing right up against one an-
other. Horror and comedy, tragedy and joy. We're bombarded with both
simultaneously, over and over again, until we can't tell where one begins
and the other ends. Until we understand, through the meditative acts of
laughing then crying and laughing and crying and laughing and crying
again, that the only thing that matters is life, now, in this moment. Is
holding on to the precious gift that is life in each moment, instead of
being a slave to the hateful agendas around us.

I think it's no accident that the core message of the film revolves around
dancing. Rosie's instruction to Jojo, by word and example, to love life
and to dance, returns to Jojo and Elsa, as they dance into the streets in
the final moments of the film. There couldn't be a more Hindu cap to
this film's lessons on life, death, comedy, and tragedy. Hinduism's Shiva,
god of consciousness and black holes, does his dance of destruction to
generate new life. Shiva is lord of the dance, and teaches his powerful
wife Shakti (an iteration of Kali and Parvati) to dance — Shakti, who is
the goddess of raw kundalini power. Kali has her own dance of death
to purge the world from its destructive demonic forces — a dance which
Shiva prevents from destroying the Earth through loving self sacrifice.

Dancing is both a metaphor for the transition between death and life,
and a literal depiction of the raw ecstatic joy of which life is comprised.

And that's what *Jojo Rabbit* is: a graphic, outrageous dance of destruction,

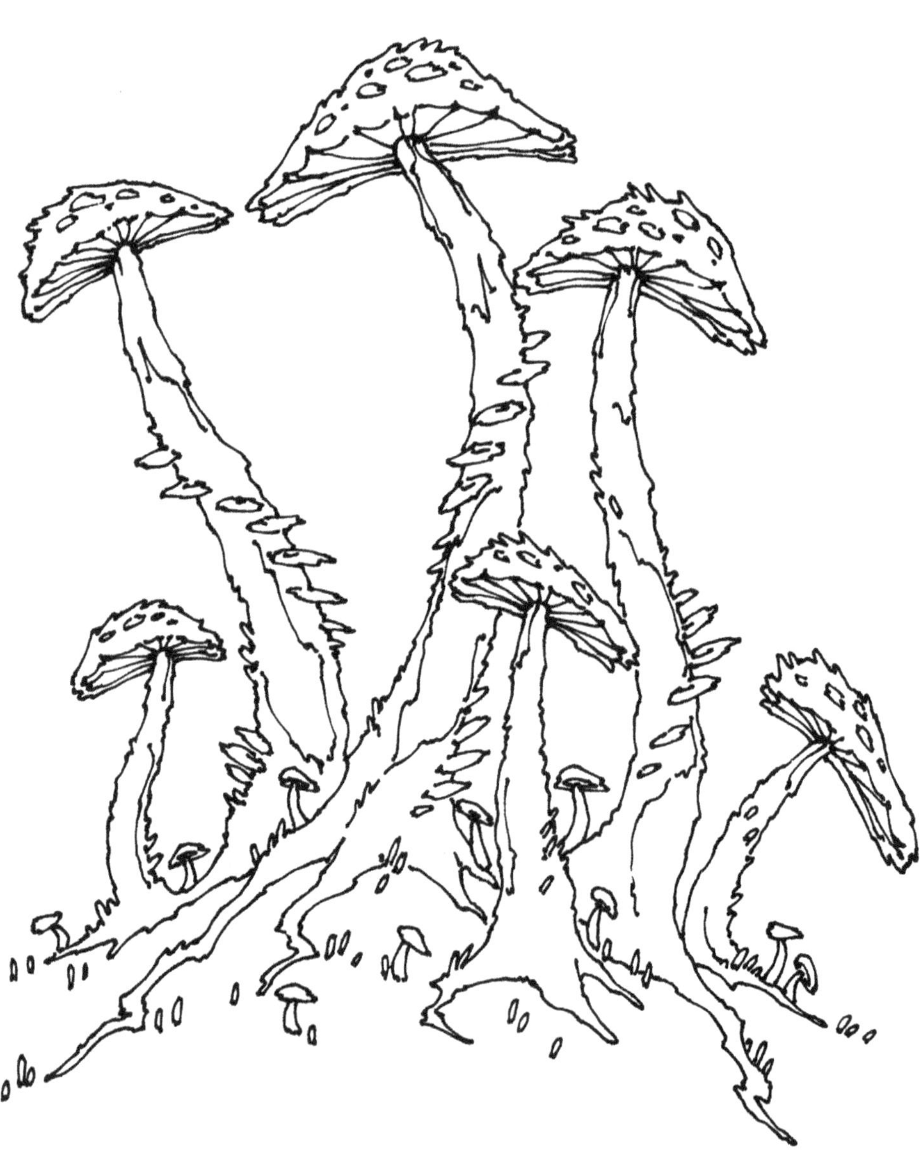

COSPOETRY

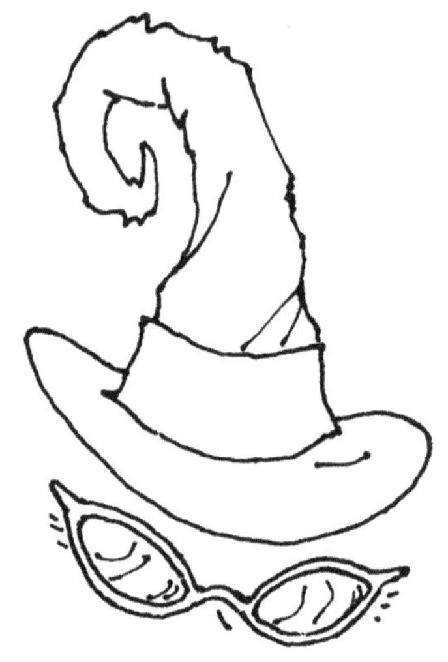

A DAY IN THE LIFE OF A MODERN WITCH

What's it like when you've lived for centuries, have magical blood that is angry, rotted and old running through your veins and are about to be late for work because you're trying to watch the latest Rihanna performance on your iPhone?

by Briana Ureña-Ravelo

Dear Diary,
Another day I wake, another day more wearied with the rotting humanity around me. It isn't their flesh that goes rancid, mind, but their hearts, so soured and bloated on the excesses of this age.

In other news, Rihanna's outfit during her performance of "Where Have You Been" at the VMAs was to DIE for!

~~~~~~~~~~~

As I walk on this street, my hand itches and I sense there is a MAN looking at me. For his own sake this is a bad idea and I will not stand for it. I will bellow and terrify the little human. Maybe then he will take care and fear for his life more.

~~~~~~~~~~~

Splitting poles is bad luck. Spilling salt is bad luck. Men in the house is bad luck.

~~~~~~~~~~~

SNEEZES THREE TIMES

Hell, someone is talking shit about me

~~~~~~~~~~~

To do list:
* Set up altar

- Glare at men
- Get that new cat food that's on sale

~~~~~~~~~~~

Holds breath while walking past Hillary Clinton's campaign office

~~~~~~~~~~~

Human: I like this little jewelry box!
Me: Thanks, it's filled with graveyard dirt, salt and a coin.

~~~~~~~~~~~

Human: What's your middle name?
Me: I don't give that out in case one of you silly fuckers tries to bind me

~~~~~~~~~~~

Dear Diary,
It seems I have misplaced my grimoire and my favorite snake ring. Today is literally the worst day ever.

~~~~~~~~~~~

Human: How has life been recently, Briana?
Me: This human body I currently inhabit has been treating me adequately, yes. I MEAN oh, this, this is mine, I was born in it, I didn't jump into the mother's womb and take her child's form when things were getting a little too heated for me in Prague! PHEW, crisis averted!

~~~~~~~~~~~

Dear Diary,
That funny little human I mentioned before just has the sweetest eyes and I am besotted with him. A love potion to gain his affection and make him leave his girlfriend would be standard fair, but of course that clearly crosses the lines of consent and isn't a sisterly way to behave to a fellow woman, who I am sure is just lovely despite being human. I shall brood in my hovel on chicken legs and work on incantations instead.

~~~~~~~~~~~

Human: Her name is Charlotte, she's two months old!
Me: Oh, she's so beautiful, can I hold her?

WHISPERING THIS TINY CHILD WILL DO, SHE HAS A STRONG AURA
~~~~~~~~~~~

~~~~~~~~~~~

Hisses and hisses and hisses and hisses and-

~~~~~~~~~~~

Dear Diary,
There is no Black sheep, wand, animal skull, or curandera emojis with the latest iOS update. Do I feel erased by Apple or would I be more offended if they engaged in what are ultimately poor, oversimplified stereotypes of my kind? #ProblematicOrNah

~~~~~~~~~~~

"Oh, I can't tonight, it's a full moon, rituals, fuckery to avoid, you know the deal!"

~~~~~~~~~~~

Looking at the moon My mother taught me that when she is yellow and half full it means she is jealous…or is it that she's in love? Either way she's sad that she lost her son.

~~~~~~~~~~~

Google Search: Does Sage Piss Off Strong Spirits?

~~~~~~~~~~~

Dear Diary,
The grumpy silver cat son across the street was kinder to me when I went to greet him today. Also, I found a nice little bird skull! It will go well with the snake skin, feathers, and wolf's skull for the altar.

~~~~~~~~~~~

Human: It's nice to have a summer party like this with staff! We should do something for the holidays!
Me: Fall is the time of the Blood Sacrifices.
Human: …yes, that's exactly what I was thinking too.
Me, ignoring human's tone: We are twins, you and I.

~~~~~~~~~~~

Dear Diary,
Rihanna in the "Pour It Up" video.

That is all.

~~~~~~~~~~~

These plants are my sons. This tiny cedar waxwing is my son. This pray-
ing mantis is my daughter. This neighborly cat is my son. All of the earth's
creatures moving and surging and birthing and dying under the eye of the
eternal heavens are my familiars and I am mother, unerring gentle yet cruel,
to them all. But to answer your question, my cat's name is Shampoo.

~~~~~~~~~~~

Dear Diary,
Tonight, I am craving a cheeseburger but have none of the wherewithal to
leave my hovel to get one.

Now truly today is literally the worst day ever.

PAUL STAMETS DREAMS OF ASTROMYCOLOGY

For the Star Fleet navigator in the IRL mycologist

by Marjorie Steele

Paul was surprised when he awoke to find
the mushroom spores had all grown iridescent
their caps a kind of neon green he'd never seen.

Nodes underground sprouted up like sunset coral
the underground being no longer ground,
but infinite space
not bound
to This Universe
or That.

In place of his Amadoo mushroom hat,
woven lovingly by ladies in Transylvania,
Paul now had ports in both forearms, and
a frozy blue glaze over his irises which would clear
and cloud, in sync with the ebb and flow of data
across the astral mycelial network.

Paul always knew he was a vessel for navigation
like the Seabear, in that the mycelium is is his natural habitat
but unlike that poor creature, in that Paul
had that spark of choice
he was willing.

"BLACK ALERT," the computer calls across the ship.

By instinct, Paul lays himself down in the spore drive chair
lays out his forearm portals,
closes his eyes,

and steps into the forest.

AVIATION MEMOIR
A galactic love poem

by johnronand

I will map the moles on your body as a constellation
that will guide the flight of my fancy and its navigation
in my exploration and revolution
round and round your heavenly body
with pure devotion
from a considerate distance
[though an osculation is bound to happen]
and in strict observance
of your beauty
and gravitation

DISC-O-WORLD

by SouthpawPoet

I was reading the news
and sipping my espresso
in a bohemian café
when suddenly my face
turned a parsnip pale
so perfect and even
no cosmetic miracle
could emulate
just by reading
what the paper said:
Earthflattener theorists
could finally demonstrate
that Gravity does not exist
and NASA videos are fake…
Then the whole alphabet
fell from the article page:
acceleration 9.8

A LOVESONG FOR JEAN LUC PICARD
And the man who makes him

by Marjorie Steele

Bodies filled the trenches
where his father fought in Normandy,
a lifetime ago

His mother's body bounced
off walls and cupboards
by bloodstained hands that just
wouldn't
wash.

His own tiny body cowered beneath
the table and cursed
himself for not being
able
to save her
to save himself.

His father couldn't save himself
from the trenches
from the bodies of his friends
from murdering young sons and fathers

His mother couldn't save herself
from her husband's dreams
from the violence against her own body
from the humiliation of joy, stolen.

He--the boy--couldn't save himself
from losing his hair too soon
not from the memory of violence
not from the crushing injustice
which flourishes along the
ragged edges of beauty.

So he became an instrument

fine-tuned himself to the Bard's lyre
and became a diplomat to the stars.

With grace and a firm command,
he brought aid to the helpless
he mediated peace between enemies
he protected the innocent
he uprooted corruption.

And when the Borg took him,
he already knew what it was
to be helpless
to be unable to save yourself —
a liability to those you love most.

When we see Picard weep, we see
a man
who understands
what it means to lack power

and is just discovering that in this
lies his deepest strength.

WINGS

by Evan Fleischer

Ornithologists at Cornell have built a bird.
They have built several.
They have built a bird that sings.
They have built a bird that dances.
They have built a series of birds that quietly watch Jonathan Franzen get
into the car every morning.
They have built a bird that wants to hire other birds to replace the tickertape
at ticker-tape parades.
Ornithologists at Cornell have assembled themselves into what they claim
is a giant bird and are slowly making their way down university halls, going,
"Squawk! Squawk!"
Car keys of the mind left to the branches,
and, 'Where are my keys?'
and — you hop, and — you point.

10 Things I Hate About Wil Wheaton

A sonnet

by Marjorie Steele

I hate the way you walk about
In your stupid little rainbow stripes
I hate the way you're such a good boyscout
You're always bitching about what's right

I hate your perfect Starfleet hair
And how you want Picard to be your dad
I hate your naive Ensign stare
And that time you crushed on a girl alien reeeeal bad

I hate the fact that Wesley Crusher was the only part
You ever really seemed to play
I hate the way you dissed Beyond and got all smart
About Jaylah's nonexistent lack of agency

But most of all I hate the way I don't hate you,
Not even close, not even a little bit, not even in season two.

2000 is 2012 is 2020

A poem for a new reality

by Nex Lelander

To everything there's a season and the season is now. The year is 2020, seed crystal for the element of time. It's as if when I wrestled with the Mayan Apocalypse with conduit poles from my little Florida rooftop in 2012 that the singularity went through my essence. And, while daybreak neared and I asked that angel a name…a reply is this moment…as all history is beamed through this 365…moving toward that hope and resolution people've always placed on the property which instances motion. It is like time lords, themselves, gain relation to human condition through pattern here. Really! British Broadcasting in some ways already acknowledges this truth. I don't know whether they'll tell you, personally, or not. But, my essence and that of Gallifrey are entwined. Who made whom, who can say? Yet, as you observed, simply reading these words, the nature of time has already changed…a series of facts I can't say anywhere. Although, I feel that they'd be safe with you…here.

FICTION

THE ULTIMATE MARVEL v DC DISS TRACK: DEADSHOT

To the tune of "Lose Yourself" by Eminem

by David Caracciolo

Forget Eminem v MGK. The ultimate rap feud is Marvel v DC! Both brands have developed strong cinematic universes. Okay… maybe not both. Marvel started it off with their successful MCU. DC tried to replicate their competition with their very own superhero team-up, Justice League…

They took aim at Marvel and missed. Now Marvel is firing back with a new diss track entitled Deadshot, to the tune of Eminem's Lose Yourself. Original song here…

Now it's your turn to sing a long…

***

DEADSHOT

Look, if you had Deadshot, one opportunity
To start a cinematic universe, in one movie
Would you Marvel it or Justice League?

Yo
His palms are sweaty, Man of Steel, arms are heavy
There's blood on his suit and cape already, Martha's thready
He's nervous, but on the surface he looks calm and ready
To drop Zod, but he keeps on forgettin'…

What Lois wrote down, the whole crowd gasps aloud
He opens his mouth, but the scream won't come out
He's chokin', how, everybody's Joker now?
The cast wants out, times up, over, KAPOW!

Snap back to reality, oh there goes Affleck
Oh, there goes Cavill, he choked
He's so mad, but he won't give up the cape, nope
He won't have it, he knows the "S" still stands for Hope…

Not Hopeless!
It don't matter,
He's out, he knows that, it's a joke
Career's stagnant, he knows
When he goes back to his mansion home, that's when it's
Back to try Bond again, this whole Witcher thing
He better shave that moustache off and "Hope" they don't pass him…

You better prove yourself in the movies, the moment
You wanted, a cinematic universe
You only get one shot, do not mess it up like Fox
Their continuity changes e-ve-ry timeline!

You better prove yourself in the movies, at the moment
You own it, you better never let it go
You only get one shot, do not get "owned" like Fox
DC's opportunity comes once in a lifetime you better… reboot?

***

Now that's what I call a Mike Drop! (Drew Pulig/Hypebeast)

You can do anything you set your mind to, DC… just not Marvel.

CONVERSATION WITH A NIGGOD #2

An Uncommon Dialogue of Real Spit about Real Shit

by Reverend Nigga Daddy

A note from the publisher: for those of you who like context, this is A Parody of Neale Donald Walsch's CONVERSATIONS WITH GOD.

***

ME: Who are You?

WON: I Am Wise, Old Nigga from da Planet Niggadom. Just call me WON for short.

ME: NIGGA is an offensive, perjorative word in this society.

Won: Its not the Word NIGGA. Its NIGGAZ, period, who are Offensive to this Society of White Patriarchal Rule also known as Rule by Stoopid White Men. Whitey taught you to be scared of a word that he claimed he invented that NIGGAZ actually invented and now every time U Negroids hear the word U git all ugly in the face.

ME: Thats heavy.

Won: Its the TRUTH. And Truth is my Religion. And I notice there is not much of Truth in your world. Mostly LIES.

ME: Well, the TRUTH HURTS.

WON: Yes. Butt the LIE KILLS.

ME: Well, Im not ready to die.

WON: Lotta Niggaz aint ready to Die. Butt try telling that to the Police.

ME: Many of my Brothaz n Sistaz in the Conscious Community have said the Word NIGGA is not fit to be used on US. They have studied linguistics extensively. So they know these things.

WON: Well, if its so DEROGATORY why do White People say it?

ME: Well, they are using it to OFFEND and CURSE us.

WON: Exactly. Except, that all words that are derived from A People who taught The WORLD to speak cannot be then USED against those SAME People. This is an Unspoken Law of Curses. Only those words which you ACCEPT as True Against You can be used Against You. This is why NIGGA wood be Offensive to You or anyone else. They are HARMED by it because they do not Recognize themselves as being from the People who are the Progenitor of All Words. When you understand this every time The ENEMY utters a word to CURSE You they have only Cursed themselves 10 times the Weight of the Intent.

ME: I be dam. I never knew this.

WON: Of course not. Most of You Niggaz here don't know this or ANYTHING, really. That's why I've been sent here to Save the 144,000 of yall that's SAVEABLE.

ME: So we should just let Whitey or whoever the ENEMY is fill the air with Niggers, Niggas n Niggaz?

WON: Um-hm...Because it will only be Ammunition Against Them—and their Offspring and their Posterity.

ME: And this will not backfire?

WON: WORDS that do not belong to you and that are TAUGHT to You cannot be Used against the Source from which they came. They automatically REVERSE THE CURSE against the Enemy who dares to try use them Against You.

ME: U learn sumpen NEW everyday.

WON: Keep an open mind.

ME: I want to git all the knowledge I kan.

WON: long as u don't become a Fool for Knowledge.

ME: Aint we sposed to learn much as possible?

WON: U really need to UNLEARN as much as possible. U need to UNLEARN what U have LEARNED so U kan RELEARN all that U have FORGOTTEN is what it is. Niggaz always tryna know MORE than da Next

Nigga and all dat do is make Niggaz wanna go round Debating otha Niggaz bout who knows da Most and What they Know. Its like A Woman who got a BIG ASS. They caint wait to Show off how BIG they knowledge base is.

ME: I thawt we were sposed to git knowledge of Self and the Universe.

WON: Well, that's what U git for Thinking. People just like to use SLO-GANS. And don't even know WHAT da SELF is.

ME: I thought it was Me.

WON: Still thinking I see.

ME: Well, what is da SELF?

***

My Niggaz: As I write this I am on the Run at the moment. Ever since the United States has made Niggaz The ENEMY of The STATE (as he said would happen) Niggaz like mah self have been Fugitives from JUST-US (Justice)..and even Just ICE (Immigration Customs Enforcement....cuz they tryna deport Niggaz again to Afrika: but more on that as mah story continues).

Bealz, Prince of the Southside: Chapter 2

The noose is set

by Gary E. Moore

Chicago sat atop the State of Illinois like a jaunty, precociously donned cap. Serving as the State's primary economic engine, amongst its greatest exports, its main contributions to the downstate economy was a steady stream of bodies to fill the many prisons spread throughout the rural areas.

And while this provided a financial boon for these sparse communities, it meant hours and hours of separation from the families they'd left behind.

It was hard enough to take the L to a real grocery store.

Many of the kids around here, where Bealz lived, were just like him. Their dads were housed in prison units hundreds of miles away. They were left behind to figure things out on their own—especially the boys. The girls tended to have more intact maternal structures, better examples. Their main problems were in fending off the well-armed, dangerously confused preteen and teenage boys raised up in a rape culture in the middle of an urban war zone.

The women then—many forced into responsibility—had no choice but to take up the mantle of leadership, not just in the home, but in the community at large. Many times, before they could even vote.

For those boys who chafed under this direction, who yearned for some greater connection to the worst of their rapidly developing instincts, there was always the streets.

There were always people like the grinning monster seated across from Bealz in the back of this one hundred thousand dollar sedan.

"What's up, lil nigga? I been tryin to catch up to you for a while."

Blinking against the unnatural darkness, Bealz can't speak. He is too afraid to move. This seems to please the man across from him.

"What you scared for, my man? I ain't gon bite."

Looking at the wet, wide smile that broke like a crack across the man's dark face, golden teeth gleaming with menace, Bealz thinks that this man is capable of doing just that. He had the look of a predator, all too willing to sink its teeth into its prey.

"I know you know me, right? Don't act like you don't. You gon hurt my feelings," the man says. His words seep into Bealz's brain, making his head hurt.

As Bealz continues to cringe against the locked car door, the man's grin melts away into a menacing sneer, "Aight now lil nigga. You hear me talkin to you. I'm tryin to be nice. To show some respect. Where's mine? I asked you a question. You know who I am?"

"Uh, yeah. I know you…," Bealz stammers hesitantly.

"What's my name?"

"Dakari," Bealz answers. The name seemed cold upon his tongue.
Sitting back, Dakari's grin returns, pleased by Bealz's answer. "Yeah. You know me."

Nodding stupidly, Bealz can feel his heart trying to burst from his chest. There is a man in the car with him. All of his senses tell him so. But Bealz can see something else. Sense something else. Something like a viscous, shifting shadow hiding just underneath.
As he stared in horror, tried to understand what he was seeing and not seeing, the pressure in his head continued to grow.

"I know you too, little man," the monster says. "Or I should probably say, I know your pops."

Taken aback, Bealz looks away from the eerie, rippling nothingness. He boldly looks at the man, the fear momentarily suspended by the mention of his father.

"Oh…," Dakari says, self satisfyingly bobbing his head. "Didn't know that, did you? Well, homeboy, let me be the first to tell you, there's a whole lot you don't know."

Dakari reaches out towards him suddenly and Bealz jumps back before seeing the gold link chain puddled in the man's outstretched palm. It had seemed to appear in his hand like some kind of magic trick.

Laughing, Dakari says, "Go head on, lil nigga. I ain't gon bite you. Shit, I can't even touch you right now. Against the rules. Later for that.

"Take the chain. It's yours."

"I'm good," Bealz blurts out, every cell in his body screaming out in panic.

The grin remains steady upon Dakari's face. Leaning closer, he says, "Take the chain."

Looking from the man's hand to his grinning, golden face, Bealz is filled with dread. The necklace seemed almost to vibrate. He could feel a menacing iciness emanating in waves from it. He wanted no part of it.

Dakari wasn't asking. Tipping his hand over, he drops the chain into Bealz's lap.

"Now get the fuck outta my car," he says, all of his charm evaporating in an instant.

When the door suddenly swings open, Bealz yelps in surprise and falls backward out onto the grimy, cinder strewn alleyway. Looking up, he sees Big Mook staring down at him. Bealz can see sunlight streaming down, around and slightly through him, as if the giant of a man were opaque.

He can see the large man's true form shifting, prismed through the sunlight. It was huge. Bealz began to struggle, trying to scrabble away from the car and the hulking monster hovering over him.

"Mook!" Dakari calls out from from black hole of a backseat. "You can touch him. Put that chain around his neck. Now!"

As the oscillating image of a man and a monster reaches down towards him, Bealz continues to scramble away, now trying to crab walk awkwardly to the side. His mouth is opened wide, as if to cry out, but he makes no sound, manages only to dumbly stare in disbelief. He understands that his reality had broken. He thought maybe he was going insane. He just wanted to get away.
He doesn't get very far.

Mook daintily plucks the chain from amid the gravelly cigarette butts and discarded detritus and gently lifts Bealz's head, cradling it like an infant in the crook of his massive arms.

Bealz can feel Mook's huge hands/talons moving with an uncharacteristic deftness across his neck, like feathers.

When Mook fastens the clasp, Bealz feels himself washing away into dark-

SOUL CATCHER #1
The life of Death as told by Dat Nigga Death

by Reverend Nigga Daddy

I knocked on da muthafuckin door.

The nigga opened it and looked me up and down n shit.

You know how Niggaz do.

Not in a Gay Way. Butt in a Do-I-Know-You-type-of-way.

In fack, dats what he said:

Do I know you?

I was like: "Nah, Mah Nigga you dont. Butt I need to talk to you."

And WHO are you lil bitty Muthafucka?

I expected him to be Suspicious.

Lets just say GOD sent Me.

See, I already knew da Nigga bleeved DEEPLY in God. Butt nobody else did. I knew doe. Cuz we keep dat type of shit on file on Niggaz. And I do mah homework before I go visit a Nigga.

A lottest of da HARDEST Niggaz in da world are either GAY—or they REAL muthafuckin RELIGIOUS. They sum God-Bleeving, God-FEAR-ING muthafuckaz. You be serprized.

They be talkin to God cuz God is da Only REAL Nigga FRIEND.

Matter-of-fack, God is da ONLY Friend of Most Real Niggaz.

Im tom bout dem type of Real Nigga MEN. The kinda Man who such a Man his womayne dont give a fuck what he do. She just love him. Cuz he a muthafuckin Man. He dont mince words. He dont apologize for shit. Just a mean muthafuckin Man. But he love his Woman. Or WOMMIN as the case may be. And they krazy bout him too. Cuz they know he

89

wood kill for em.

Yet, he real muthafuckin religious down Deep.

So I knew dat when I said GOD it wood TRIGGER NAPOLEAN LAMAR JENKINS, THE THIRD (III)….Aka NAPS. Also known as The GENER-AL.

NAPS stood up wit all his height. Nigga was tall 6'6". Big Nigga.

In mah line of work I have to come to find out dat a lotta real mean, niggaz are BIG Niggaz. Or Small Niggaz. A small Nigga hoo take up a lotta space tho. I knew a muthafucka like dat. I will tell you bout Him in anutha one of mah stories. I had to go talk to him too.

Butt anyway so Im talking to da Big Nigga, NAPS.

And I said Yeah God sent me.

And he was like: "Hmmm. What do you MEAN, Nigga?"

I said look Brotha. You dont know me. Butt God knows YOU."

You a Passa or Minister or sumpen?

You cood say dat.

What do you do?

Well most of the time I give LAST RITES.

LAST RITES? What you mean, Muthafucka?

You know. When A Nigga is DEAD. When he DIE, I say da Last Words over da Muthafucka.

Awww, you one dem Muthafuckaz I saw in a movie do dat shit.

Yeah.

What you want, Nigga. Aint nobody EVER said nuthin bout No mutha-fuckin GOD to me. What you know bout dat?!

And just like dat I was IN da apartment. And I was talkin to him.

I tole da Nigga in a nutshell dat he had 2 weeks to live.

He looked at me like I was krazier than-a-muthafucka. Reached for his Burner n shit. But he just putt his HAND on da muthafucka.

I didnt even Flinch. I just kept laying back smoking da Blunt we had started smokin—and drankin sum Amsterdam Vodka straight out da Bottle n shit.

Then he said: FOURTEEN muthafuckin DAYS, huh? 14 Day Notice?

I said: Yeah, Mayne. You got 14 days to live on God's Green Earth if you Dont STOP living the fucked up life you living, Mah Nigga.

And what kind of Life is dat?

Lets just say GOD know. And you DAM sho know.

I had to keep TRIGGERING da Nigga wit God. Cuz dats da onliest Muthafucka he Believed and Trusted. If I had said it was ME telling him he whudden have given a fuck.

Umph, He said. Imma DO IT.

He LIED. They All Do. 14 Days later I was da last thang he saw before his Soul rushed outta him and I had to grab it. Before it got back to God.

I had tole him GOD.

Butt I LIED Too.

I actually I work for MYSELF.

Im the SOUL COLLECTOR.

And I Collect Souls.

Sum call Me DEATH. Thats actually Better.

What I DO wit da Souls is why I stay in bizness.

I will tell you mo about dat lata doe.

Meanwhile, when I cum see you, you got TWO WEEKS to git yo shit together. And LIVE. Or DIE.

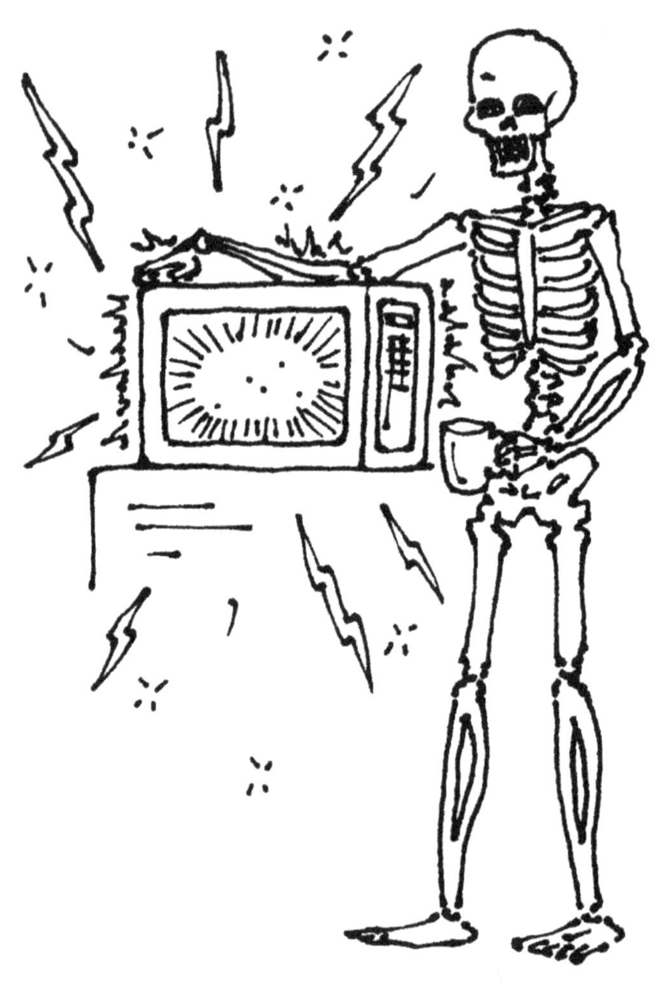

TECH SABBATICAL
A deindustrial short

by Gary E. Moore

"…Dad? What is this?"

"It's dinner. Now eat it, Zajre. Stop complaining. All of you."

Clearing his throat politely, Armaine, the youngest of Eugene's current brood of children, and definitely the more thoughtful of the bunch, points out what should be obviously apparent to their suddenly confusing father.

"Uhm, Dad? You do realize that this device uses a potentially harmful wave of radiation to corrupt the atomic structure of the very foodstuffs you intend for us to eat now don't you?"

"What? This microwave?" Eugene asks with incredulity.

"Son, these were utilized for more than a century. They were everywhere. Everyone's home was equipped with these. Most were even more powerful than this one."

"That's not comforting, Dad," Marcel, the second born of the current brood says with sullen indignity. "The 20th and 21st Centuries were filled with idiots."

"Well, those idiots eventually led us to where we are today, so something must've worked out right. Right?"

"That's a dumb argument, Pops," says Marcel.

"Well, give me a better one."

"Oh, I got this," Zajre harrumphs with certainty. "You've had us poppin' shots full of Google knows what for weeks now. And for what? You don't think I know?

"This stuff is full of poisons and carcinogens, isn't it?"

"I knew it! You were immunizing us from 21st Century pollutants so you could bring us all the way up here in the middle of know-where just so you could have your darned 'tech sabbatical'. Now, I'm completely cut off! My EyeGlass isn't even online! I can only see you in 3Dimensions! Mom totally knew what you were doing!"

"Wow, Zajre, that's more than you've said all weekend," Eugene retorts.

"Fine with me," snorts Marcel.

"Shut up, Dork! You only say that cuz you got no one linked to your accounts."

"Do too!"

"Doo Doo!"

"Enough, you two. Now come on, this stuff isn't going to hurt you. It's actually supposed to be quite tasty."

"Uh-uhn, Dad!" Armaine says pensively. "I'm not gonna eat this. I don't think any of us should. Is that meat? Real meat?"

"You bet! Your Uncle Top has a buddy who still maintains a genetic line. Stuffs expensive, but I really wanted to give you guys the total experience."

"Oh, Dad," Armaine says, shaking his head pityingly. "I think you're having a bit of a mid-millennial crisis. You're coming up on, what, your 4th century. What are we? Your fifth brood?"

"Starting to feel a touch of nostalgia, are we?"

"Shut up, Smart Ass! Not everyone gets to hang out with their kids on milestone birthdays."

"Dad," Zajre says sympathetically. Or perhaps it's simply exasperation?

"What does any of this have to do with getting old? Irradiated meat? That's only gonna make you feel older. And did these vegetables come out of that metal container?"

"It smells metally, or something, doesn't it?"

Eugene, growing ever more exasperated, growls, "Does not! Geesh! I'm not trying to put this into your daily diets. Just once isn't gonna kill you!"

"Allegedly." Marcel deadpans.

"Look," Eugene says with finality. "This isn't the first time I've eaten this. Hell, back when I was your age, this was it! The Corporate State had seized the food chain and everything was delivered in a non-biodegradable package!"

"Sounds horrible," Zajre says truthfully.

"Well, it wasn't. And it was wonderful."

"…and also gene-altering, carcinogenic, environmentally disruptive and socially unsustainable…," Armaine ponders.

"Enough, already!"

"Does that mean we won't have to eat it?"

Eugene, slowly lowering himself to rest upon the non-reactive counter top, buries his head in his hands.

This was going to be a long two weeks.

Just wait until he shows them the lawn darts, he thinks.

"…no…that's not what I meant…"

TRESPASSERS: CHAPTER I
A meeting of old friends

by Bill Henning

The sun peeked over the horizon, burning away the dark grey sky of night and bleeding the orange rays of warmth onto the town of Puntarenas, Costa Rica. The light began to crawl its way up into Scott Richards' small hotel room. He loved the sight of the sunrise in Costa Rica. Honestly, he loved a lot about Costa Rica—the sights, the beaches, the food, the women—and the number of people willing to look the other way and help smuggle someone to an island about 120 miles off the coast. For the right amount of money, of course.

Richards had missed Costa Rica dearly, but the Costa Rican government did not miss him. Due to these previously mentioned activities, Richards was slapped with several lawsuits from some very powerful people inside a company known as InGen, also known as International Genetics Incorporated. At the time—eight years ago now—they were on the cutting edge of technology, and one of the most powerful companies on the planet. Their army of gorillas in suits (also known as lawyers) took every cent Richards had and forced the Costa Rican government to more or less ban him from the country.

The icing on the InGen cake was that technically he was an employee of theirs and had done a lot of startup work in the '80s around two islands off the US Pacific coast. He was personally asked by the man who founded InGen, John Hammond, to help with mapping and surveying an island for "a project that would change the world!"

That's how Hammond put it. A few years later, Hammond called on Richards again to do the same thing to another island, saying it would be the main attraction. Richards surveyed the island.

It wasn't until years later that Richards found out what Hammond was up to, and he couldn't believe his eyes. Sadly, the way he found out was also how the lawyers got involved, and Richards never got to see John Hammond again before he died two years ago. It was one of the biggest regrets of Richards' life. The old man was always a joy to be around, and despite the falling out between Richards and InGen, Richards always felt the rift had never been between him and Hammond.

Right before his death, the whole world found out about the island and the inhabitants of genetically modified, walking, breathing, living dinosaurs. How everyone found out was a bit of a disaster, to say the least. One of the dinosaurs—a big one—got loose in San Diego in 1997, which caused the death of quite a few people. That was the last straw for InGen. They went bankrupt; Richards had no idea what happened to the island and the dinosaurs after that, as he was still banned by the government of Costa Rica.

Until about a month ago, when he received a message that he was able to enter the country under some strict rules. He was to go to Puntarenas only and to meet someone and talk about a business opportunity, which set off about half a dozen alarms in Richards mind.

Puntarenas? So close to Isla Nublar seemed a little odd, but he took the opportunity anyways. Richards was in Istanbul as part of a team to survey the Black Sea for some shipwreck when the funds ran out. Richards was out of a job and didn't see the harm in hearing out who ever asked him to come back to Costa Rica.

The only instructions that were left for him at his hotel were that Richards was going to meet his possible future employer for an early lunch. Richards had gotten in yesterday late, making it a little difficult for him to reach out to his old contacts as he'd planned to this morning. Old friends might have information to fill him in on what he was doing in Puntarenas again.

Richards slipped on his khaki pants and off-white safari button up shirt, leaving a few buttons open, as he knew the heat and humidity would overtake the day. Richards rolled up his sleeves. He didn't dare take on Puntarenas with shorts and a t-shirt, as he knew the mosquitoes would eat him alive. Locking the wooden door, Richards took off to see some old faces.

***

Midday, and the sun was beating down on Richards as he sat in a flimsy metal chair outside of a small restaurant near the water. He took a long sip from his beer—it was some light cheap beer that the restaurant had, and he was purposely drinking it fast before it got warm in this weather. It worked well enough to wash down what the restaurant called "food."

Across the table from Richards was a beautiful woman dressed in a light khaki pant suit and a powder blue shirt underneath; her blonde hair was up in a ponytail and she wore a rather expensive pair of Ray-Ban sunglasses. Richards had taken off his aviator sunglasses when he sat down to eat, but the woman, who still hadn't given her name yet, did not. She was all business, and she was waiting until Richards was finished to continue with her sales pitch, never taking her hand off of a dark leather briefcase she had next to her chair.

Richards sat his beer on the table and looked around the area at people sitting and eating, seagulls bothering everyone, and the sound of the waves crashing against the coast. Finally he turned to the business woman and waited for her to say something.

"Are you ready to start?" She said after a moment.
"Sure," Richards said sipping his beer again.
"You were 18 when John Hammond first approached you right?"
"Yes."

Richards raised an eyebrow at this--straight to Hammond? So it has to do with InGen again, and the islands.

"You must have been something special for…"
"Before you continue," Richards said cutting her off, "I have to tell you there are about a dozen international laws I would be breaking if I talked to you about Isla Nublar."

"I know," she said as she started to pull folders out of her leather brief-case. "But that is why my employer brought you here to talk about the island."

"If you want someone to get you onto the island I know some people," Richards started in, testing the water to see why this nice looking busi-nesswoman wanted to know about Isla Nebular. "In fact there is a guy, Enrique. Real good guy is setting up a sort of tourism thing with para-gliding near Isla Sorna. Should have it up and running within a year, he said."

Richards took a long drink from his cheap beer. The woman didn't look entertained, but annoyed—maybe because Richards took her off her track? Richards put his beer down on the table and gave it a beat before continuing.

"Look, I don't know who is left from InGen, but I really don't want to deal with any of their lawyers anymore or what's his name….Ludlow? Hammond's asshole nephew."

"Peter Ludlow is dead," she said bluntly, pulling out a folder that had Richards' name on it.
"He is?"
"He was killed by a Tyrannosaurus Rex in San Diego."

Richards gave half a laugh as he picked up the beer bottle again. Well, at least this little meeting wasn't completely pointless; that was the best news he had gotten in years.

"As for the rest of the lawyers InGen had, I am all that is left," the woman said. "You can call me Doyle."

She reached out her hand for Richards to shake; he did but was skeptical.

"First or last name?" Richards asked.

"Last," Doyle said.

"Okay…"

"Let's also get this out of the way: I was lead on your InGen case, essentially the reason why you were never allowed to go back to the island and banned from Costa Rica."

"Oh," Richards said. "Nice to know."

"Better you hear it from me than you finding out later," she said. "Back to Hammond; why did he pick you at age 18? You seem a little young to map out an uncharted island."

"Hammond said he knew raw talent when we saw it." Richards said looking out at the water. "I had a good eye and a good hand for mapping, he offered me a job that paid well and an exotic locale to work at…What would you have done?"

"I would have taken the job," Doyle said plainly.

"Exactly."

"That was Isla Sorna?"

"Yes," Richards answered. "Some years later he asked me to do Nublar. Of course I accepted. I enjoyed working for Hammond; he was a happy old man, like he should have been playing Santa at some mall."

Doyle gave a half smirk.

"You signed an NDA," Doyle stated. Richards noticed it wasn't a question.

"Yes," Richards said.

"And your original contract stated you couldn't come back to Nublar until the construction was done. So why did you sneak onto the island….five different times?"

"Curiosity," he said, "Didn't hear back from Hammond or InGen in years I wanted to know what they were up to. Who knew that crazy old bastard would be doing the impossible."

He leaned in to whisper to her at this point.

"Jurassic Park. Dinosaurs," he said with a smile. "Very cool stuff."

"You would have found out just like everyone else," Doyle said.

"No I wouldn't. Park was closed before it even opened."

"Do you want to go back?" Doyle asked as she handed him a folder with a logo on it reading MASRANI. "My employer has a very small window and needs your help."

BONUS COMIC!

Comic for Zombies
got brains?
Dude...
Road trip to the city!
VRRRRRRR

BY ILLUSTRATOR DUSTIN COON!

Wait, we can't drive!
We're zombies!
Oh fuck!
You're right—
BAM!
END
comic by dustin coon x hydriumstudio.com

Get More COSGRRRL!

Catch all the issues from COSGRRRL's Elemental Series:

Issue #1: Origins

Issue #2: Mind / Air

Issue #3: Body / Earth

Issue #4: Emotion / Water

Issue #5: Spirit / Fire

and other great titles by Creativeonion Press at https://creativeonionpress.com.

For wholesale purchasing, please email press@creativeonion.me.

To purchase more of Dustin Coon's artwork, visit https://hydriumstudio.com.

ABOUT COSGRRRL:

COSGRRRL is nerd literary magazine which fights evil by talking about what we love. We believe the nerdier genres are genetically engineered to fight evil, because they turn our conversations towards unity, justice, equality, hope, respect, and they challenge the blind abuse of technology. Sci-fi and fantasy teach us to ask "what if?" - and they show us that when we are unified in our diversity, we are strong. Online at COSGRRRL.com, we publish content in five categories: essays, reviews, humor, cospoetry, and (fan+) fiction. Editorial guidelines revolve around one rule: You love what you love. What we want to know is: Why?

Marjorie Steele is a writer, journalist, and educator who's lived in the Midwest only *most* of her life. A chronic essayist and poet, Marjorie has pounded the beat on local issues of homelessness and urban development for Issue Media, and has reported on cannabis nationally for Leafly. Her poetry has been awarded by the Dyer-Ives Poetry Competition (2017), and her journalistic work was published in Belt Publishing's "Grand Rapids Grassroots: An Anthology" in 2017. In addition to publishing COSGRRRL, Marjorie hosts her works and private conversations at the @creativeonion network at https://network.creativeonion.me.

Dustin Coon is creator/owner of Hydrium Studio, a platform for illustration, writing & design projects. As an illustrator, his journey has been spent investing time and clarity around nature, consciousness & the cosmos. His biggest project is a sci-fi graphic novel series, "Warped Over", telling an epic tale between father & son, after their colony of humans warped through a blackhole into a highly advanced alien galaxy with no return. More great art, comics, projects, commissions & good vibes >> www.hydriumstudio.com / @hydriumstudio